designing women

Woody Allen
Eric Lax
FOUR LIVES IN PARIS
PARIS WAS A WOMAN
WIFE DRESSING BY ANNE FOGARTY
DIANA VREELAND
Writers Houses

designing women

Interiors by Leading Style Makers

Margaret Russell

Photographs by John M. Hall

Foreword by Martha Stewart

Stewart, Tabori & Chang
NEW YORK

contents

for

eword

Throughout recorded history there have always been a few outstanding women famous for their style, their personal expression, their beauty, their intellect and their appeal. In this group I would of course include Hatshepsut, the only female pharaoh, who built a palace in the Valley of the Queens that was so outstanding that it is still considered a wonder of design, location, and decoration, and a landscaping feat. Diane de Poitiers, the mistress of Henry I of France, was not only a spectacular beauty, an intellectual and athletic creature, she also understood grand design, fine craftsmanship, and pure luxuriousness. Empress Wu of the Tang Dynasty was thoroughly interested in the home and garden. She is credited with popularizing the Tree Peony and bringing its image into Chinese art and fabric. Catherine the Great assembled a court of immense interest, and many of the world's most recognizable buildings and fascinating *objets d'art* were constructed and created during her long reign. Elizabeth I was another monarch who ruled long and spent a great deal of time and effort on the construction of amazing things. Victoria, queen, wife, mother, explored the world through the travels of her explorers and Lords and collected many of its treasures. She mothered a style all her own that was influential all over the globe and prominent for ages.

These are just some of the famous women I think of when I contemplate design and style, but of course there has always been the lesser known woman, the homemaker, who in her own inimitable way creates a place of comfort, beauty, and interest for her loved ones. It is she who surrounds her family with furniture, gardens, color, and warmth. She looks to others for inspiration and education. She reads books and magazines and visits museums and historic restorations for ideas and creative solutions for everyday problems. She studies interior decorating and architecture and landscape design, and every so often one of these women becomes famous for her own style. This book is about them, the professionals. I think you will find the group diverse. I think you will like what they have done, not just in their professional lives but also personally, living what they preach, what they design, and what they have centered their careers on.

—Martha Stewart

desi

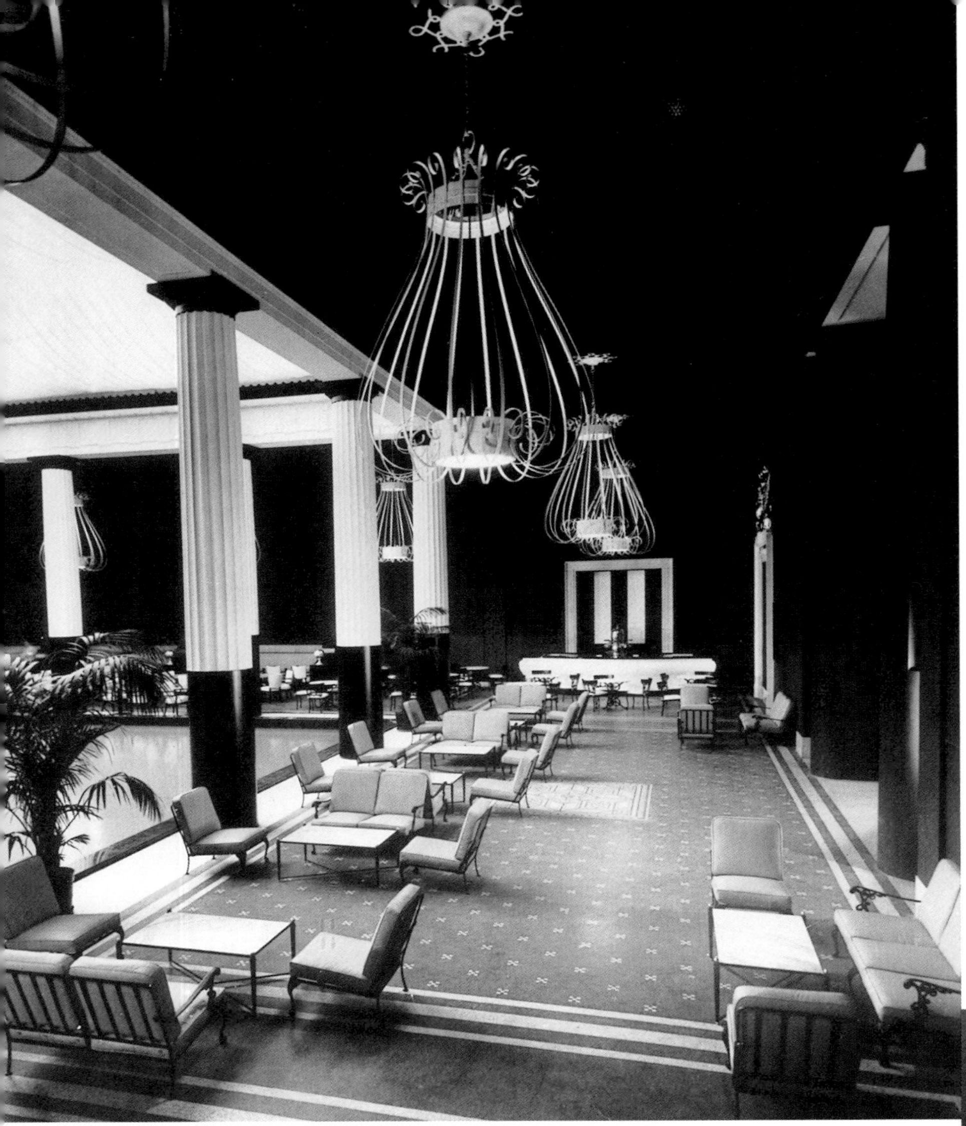

gn legacy

This is a book about women for women. The sixteen featured style makers have truly mastered the art of living well. All are confident, successful people whose accomplishments in design and the way they choose to live can both influence and inspire. Only eight are professional interior decorators; one is an architect. The balance are women with exceptional taste who are central to the world of design. They carry on the legacy of trailblazing forebears such as Elsie de Wolfe, Dorothy Draper, Frances Elkins, Madeleine Castaing, Rose Cumming, and Sister Parish, pioneer decorators who brought warmth and style to homeowners around the world.

Rose Cumming once wrote of the "artistic alchemy" that enables someone to transform a house into a home: "No amount of training or schooling can teach you this. Either you have flair or you haven't." The women featured in *Designing Women* definitely have flair. Better yet, each has a sense of humor and a healthy dose of joie de vivre. Their homes reveal that there is no single way to decorate and that good taste needs no passport and has no price tag. These extraordinary, creative women have inspired me. I hope they will encourage you, too, to live in a more thoughtful, more meaningful manner in a home that expresses your own personal style.

—Margaret Russell

CLOCKWISE FROM TOP LEFT

Dorothy Draper's design for the cafeteria at New York's Metropolitan Museum of Art; Draper, circa 1930; Edward Steichen's portrait of Elsie de Wolfe, originally published in *Vogue* in 1924; Sister Parish, photographed by Horst P. Horst.

Interior designer Suzanne Rheinstein knows how to live well. Like any successful decorator, she has a keen appreciation for the simple luxuries that make life more comfortable for her demanding client list. Yet Rheinstein's own house—a gracious early twentieth-century Georgian Revival in Los Angeles's tony Hancock Park—and her style of entertaining there best exemplify her true talent: creating a life rich in warmth and comfort.

Although famous for the stylish ease with which she entertains, Rheinstein says, "How you live your life every day is so much more important than getting your house together for a special occasion or holiday." Adamant about not being afraid to use precious things—silver, crystal, linens, china—every day, she runs what many would consider a rather formal house with a refreshingly breezy lack of pretense.

suzanne r

heinstein

PRECEDING PAGE **In the living room, painted Chinese wallpaper from Fred Rheinstein's childhood home, eighteenth-century oil paintings of Venetian doges, and a nineteenth-century neoclassical Italian chest.**

LEFT **A pair of Directoire armchairs, circa 1800, flank the eighteenth-century English carved mantel; Rheinstein upholstered the rosewood Regency daybed in a silk-and-linen stripe by Robert Kime.**

"Ages ago, I had a design epiphany," she says. "I read a *Los Angeles Times* profile in which the interviewer was getting rather personal with the writer Joan Didion, whom I greatly admire, chiding her for using her good silver at the table every day, to which she replied something like 'Why not? Everyday is all there is.' 'Everyday is all there is,' that's my mantra. I carried that clipping around forever until it finally disintegrated!"

Formerly a television producer of everything from news and documentaries to talk shows and cooking segments, the designer moved to L.A. after marrying Fred Rheinstein, also a television-industry veteran, almost twenty years ago. Seven-and-a-half months pregnant when she produced her last show, she chose not to return to television after giving birth to their daughter, Kate. Instead, she turned her talents to volunteer work, including community garden projects and historic-preservation efforts.

Rheinstein's love of interior design grew from the renovation of her own house, as well as from her lifelong interest in history, architecture, and the decorative arts. The 1916 Georgian-style brick structure, built at a time of prosperity and attention to detail, features rooms generous in scale with understated ornamentation. The entry hall, which boasts a grand piano and deep red walls, leads to a spacious square living room, an intimate library and breakfast room, a generous dining room, and a newly renovated butter-yellow kitchen and serving area.

The rooms are decorated with a mix of antiques and *objets* culled from trips abroad and family homes in Louisiana and New York. In the living room, the carved marble mantel came from Fred's childhood home, a traditional townhouse on Manhattan's Upper East Side. "We're fortunate to have been given some beautiful things by our families, and to have

traveled and brought back pieces we love," Rheinstein says, "but the trick is to use them in a more casual way." Oriental carpets from Fred's family are layered one atop another, antique side chairs are tucked into corners, garden flowers and branches are loosely arranged in unexpected containers, such as a porcelain tureen or a silver-plate Regency urn.

Rheinstein, born and raised in New Orleans, religiously adheres to the "Come on in, we're having a party" enthusiasm of her native city, entertaining at least once a week. She regularly throws events relating to Hollyhock and Hollyhock Hilldale, her two antiques and design shops, as well as for the Los Angeles Conservancy, the Decorative Arts

ABOVE **The dining-room walls were glazed in translucent stripes. Rheinstein hung an antique Swedish mirror over an eighteenth-century Italian console; the silver is Sheffield, the porcelain is a mix of Chinese export china and English lustreware.**

Council of the Los Angeles County Museum of Art, the Library Council, and other local institutions that she and her husband support.

Whether at a casual fireside supper served on trays or a blowout book party for a visiting author, guests are made to feel welcome the moment they arrive: the air is fragrant, music is playing, candles are scattered throughout the house, votives and lanterns illuminate the garden. "I've never been daunted by having people over," Rheinstein says. "Just make simple food and have lots of it, and put out a million candles. Candles hide a multitude of sins.

"I can't tell you the last time I gave a sit-down dinner in my dining room, the way I did when we were first married," Rheinstein says. "We are so much more casual now." Large dinners are buffet-style, not seated, with stacks of different patterns of antique porcelain plates, scores of antique silver forks, and rows of vintage banquet-sized linen napkins. Free to explore the house and gardens, Rheinstein's guests often end up in her latest renovation, a garden room at the end of a brick path. Formerly a chauffeur's cottage, the double-height, wainscoted pavilion has floor-to-ceiling French doors, which open onto a swimming pool and the designer's remarkable gardens.

The gardens were carefully plotted out, inspired both by those seen abroad and by local Pacific horticulture. "We used to have a free-form pool that took up the backyard," Rheinstein says. "It took me seventeen years to talk my husband into changing it, so I seized the opportunity to redo the gardens." In addition to such favorites as a "fabulous salvia black-and-blue," sedum, verbascum, zonal geraniums, and pots of succulents, her cutting garden includes "pale, pale old-fashioned roses for the house," red flowers for the breakfast room, and green- and black-eyed Susans for the kitchen.

OPPOSITE **Rheinstein upholstered the walls in the front hall in a Scalamandré damask and framed the doors in narrow red grosgrain ribbon. The dining-room chandelier is early-nineteenth-century Russian, the sideboard is eighteenth-century English. The Regency dining table is set for a New Orleans brunch of grillades and cheese grits.**

The library looks out over the more formal garden, punctuated by gravel paths, a small, round reflecting pond, and a secret garden in its infancy, with hedges just beginning to fill out. "Fred wanted a crisp garden," Rheinstein says. "He didn't want to look out and see a mad cottage garden. So, I planned this garden to fit in with the style of the house, and I think it works well; it's green and serene and quiet. It's amazing to be able to live as urban as you can in Los Angeles and yet have this enormously private space barely a mile south of the Hollywood sign. I just love that."

OPPOSITE **Rheinstein mixed a dusky apple-green paint for the walls of her breakfast room. The wing chairs are slipcovered in a large-scale Brunschwig & Fils floral linen; the Regency chairs are covered in a crisp black-and-cream stripe. Vintage French confiture jars and blue-and-white Chinese cricket boxes are used as candle holders.**

ABOVE **In the butler's pantry, the original bottom cabinets were retrofitted with pull-out drawers to store stacks of china; a rolling library ladder accesses the top shelves. Rheinstein renovated the kitchen but kept the remarkable original stove.**

'''Everyday is all

there is,' that's my mantra"

LEFT **In the garden room, the sofa is upholstered in coral-striped Indian cotton. The refectory table is a North Carolina antique dating from the 1860s; the pagodas and rattan chair are from Hollyhock. Rheinstein painted the French doors a glossy dark green-black.** FOLLOWING PAGES **Counterclockwise from top left, the Beebe rattan chaise longues are from Hollyhock; exotic succulents flourish in prim Regency planters. Moonflowers curtain an arch that shelters a reproduction Lutyens chair. Rheinstein painted a vintage iron table in her favorite chartreuse-and-black stripes; the English armchair is from Treillage.**

design details

- use masses of candles, all over the house. I use beeswax: cream candles for summer, black for winter
- collect large napkins, old and new, damask or linen, with others' monograms or with your own. They'll cover your entire lap like a personal tablecloth
- mix up your old crystal and china for parties rather than renting matching sets. My neighbors and I borrow silver from each other for really large gatherings
- collect beautiful, oversized old forks if you like to serve buffet-style
- if you entertain often, consider buying extra ballroom chairs, the classic bamboo style. Some friends and I purchased thirty chairs that we share; we just store them in my attic
- serve delicious food that is homemade—or that could be. Solution? Give the caterer your family recipes
- don't rely on stiff, formal floral arrangements. Use flowers that look as if they came straight from the garden

"I find myself doing things here I would never do anywhere else," says Holly Hunt of her home away from home—a romantic two-bedroom Paris pied-à-terre in the eighth arrondissement near the place de la Madeleine. Not only does she sleep later, eat later, and walk five times as much, she says, "I go to the neighborhood croissant shop and flower market on Saturday; it's a whole different lifestyle. There's something about the rhythm of being in Paris, and there's no city more beautiful, period."

Hunt, primarily a Chicago resident, owns an influential eponymous showroom of contemporary design with branches across the United States. In particular, her representation of the French furniture designer Christian Liaigre in the mid-1990s popularized a modern, minimalist approach that has had enormous influence on both residential and commercial interiors today.

holly

hunt

Four years ago, with business taking her to Paris every couple of months, Hunt took over the apartment of Christian Astuguevielle, a designer she also represents. "He was moving to another apartment in the building and suggested that I take his old one." She did, promptly renovating the kitchen and baths, and asked Astuguevielle to replicate some of his previous decor for her, notably some pieces of his signature cord-wrapped furniture. The French, Hunt says, "value the decorative arts—objects and furniture and the history of them. In the States, if you tire of it, you often just get rid of it."

The apartment, which was constructed in the early nineteenth century and retains its original details, has been pushed into the present, though with sensitivity. "You need to fit the scale, the size of the rooms," Hunt says, explaining her reliance on simple, strong-lined furniture—much of it designed for the space by Liaigre and Astuguevielle—and a warm but limited palette of soft blacks, oatmeal tones, and earthenware greens.

In the petit salon, for instance, where she works and has small dinners, a black-lacquer Chinese table stands in one corner, banked by matching stools cushioned in kick-pleated linen that echoes the color of a massive cord-wrapped Astuguevielle settee nearby. Her bedroom is equally restrained, all white linen and framed turn-of-the-century sepia photographs. And instead of taking Liaigre's advice to hang voluminous curtains in brilliant jewel tones—claiming, "Holly, you need color in your life"—Hunt installed panels of citrine-colored silk at nearly every window. "I can only deal with one color," she says with a laugh, "and I've never had a house where I've had curtains in every room, but this place just demands curtains."

It also demanded proper bathrooms, American-style. In typical

PRECEDING PAGE **The grand salon in Holly Hunt's Paris pied-à-terre is dominated by a trio of overscaled slip-covered club chairs and a sofa by Belgian antiques dealer and furniture master Axel Vervoordt. The wood-and-leather side chair is by Christian Liaigre.** OPPOSITE **Hunt designed the grand salon's rosewood stereo cabinet; its doors are faced in vellum. The painting is by Sean Scully.**

E.PRINTZ
FRANK

"There's something about the rhythm
there's no city

of being in Paris, and more beautiful, period"

LEFT **In the petit salon, a nineteenth-century lacquered Chinese dining table and stools. Hunt preserved the intricate Louis-Philippe architectural detail throughout the apartment and painted the walls and moldings a chalky white. The herringbone chestnut parquet floors were stripped and sealed in a matte finish.**

ABOVE **The lacquer-and-white oak library table was made by Liaigre for the grand salon; the vase is 1920s French; the drawing is by Hans Hoffman. Blossoms float in a shallow tray in front of a tufted settee by designer Christian Astuguevielle.**

OPPOSITE **The enfilade from the grand salon to the petit salon. Billowing curtains throughout the apartment add a tailored yet feminine touch; made of silk, they are an ethereal citrine bordered in a wide swath of bronze.**

French fashion, "It had a tub and a sink where the master bath is normally, and the toilet was all the way around on the other side of the apartment," recalls Hunt. The chestnut herringbone floors were stripped and given a quiet matte finish. The architectural elements—"cake-icing" is how Hunt describes the high-relief plaster swags and moldings—were calmed down, too, with a wall-to-wall coat of parchment white. "Making everything one color modernizes it a bit. It still has this sense of French history, but for an American, it works well, too."

FRANK

OPPOSITE AND ABOVE **In the kitchen, Christian Astuguevielle created the table, lattice-back chairs, and dramatic sideboard faced in his signature wrapped cording. The chestnut cabinet and plate rack are also his designs.**

FOLLOWING PAGES **From left, the Brancusi-inspired table in Hunt's dressing room is by Liaigre; the shelves, drawers, and floors look as if they are leather-covered but are actually faced in lacquered MDF laminate board. White linen curtains the wall behind Hunt's bed. A framed series of 1890s photographs of Greek ruins provide a counterpoint to the paneled walls in the bedroom's sitting area.**

design details

- the French collect things and keep things and then resell them; it's a flea-market mentality. There is an abundance of decorative-arts objects there because they don't toss them out
- the joy of having a second house is being able to make it look different from the place you live most of the time. Try something new: it's boring if your houses look the same and only the landscapes are different
- my favorite luxury is going to sleep on really good sheets. Now that my children are grown, I don't feel guilty buying Pratesi linens and having them sent out to be washed and pressed; there's nothing better
- the furnishings in a house should be indigenous to that space. A boiserie-covered room should not have the same decor as an apartment in a modern glass tower. It's not just the period, it's also the scale—the size of the rooms and the height of the ceilings
- nothing is superior to white linen fabric when you want something simple
- refinished antiques look all dressed up and ready to go to a party. It's better if they look aged and used.

tricia

Color is designer Tricia Guild's claim to fame and the key element in her spacious London home, which she considers "a design lab as I work with new colors and ideas." Also, adds Guild, known for her vibrant Designers Guild fabrics and accessories, Kings Road design emporium, and numerous books for the home, "It's a very important part of my work, to actually do what I'm telling everybody else to do, which is to live in a personally expressive environment."

Curiously, though the designer's passion is for courageous colors, her home, in the trendy Notting Hill area of London, is outwardly restrained and proper, a typical Victorian row house of leaf-brown brick and creamy stucco. Sadly, the house had been stripped of much of its charm by the time Guild discovered it six years ago. "It was a total wreck. Only a few details remained, like the arch in the hallway, which was half

guild

there, so I put that back, and the cornice of the sitting room," she says. The absence of prominent baseboards and moldings, however, allowed her more freedom of choice. "I felt that I almost had a clean palette in which I could work."

Originally divided into separate floor-through apartments—"not terribly beautiful, as you can imagine," Guild says with a laugh—the house is now a single residence again. Though the background of the rooms is fairly neutral (wood and stone floors, white ceilings, and white plaster walls), and the furniture (modern English and Italian seating spiced with ethnic antiques) remains fairly constant, Guild's environment is nonetheless an ever-altering album of color, pattern, and texture.

Chez Guild, things come and go. "I'm committed to a contemporary lifestyle," the designer says, adding, "I'm a romantic, but I'm not nostalgic." A previously white wall might be roughly sponged with a coat of dazzling Caribbean blue paint, as in the living room, or a fireplace surround dressed in lime green, or a white-linen chair appear newly lilac. Slipcovers glide on and off, colorful candles are set on trays, and heavy curtains go up in the winter and come down in the spring when they are replaced with light, unlined fabrics. In the dining room, however, curtains are nowhere to be found, just a dramatic wall of glass offering a view of the gravel-paved garden and leafy arbor.

"I'm quite disciplined, in a scatty sort of way," the designer says of her home's relaxed atmosphere of refined improvisation. At the moment, the living room combines heavy washed linen with artfully worn velvets, and spiky flowers—purple, green, blue—punctuate tabletops with instant shots of pure color. Throughout the house are exotic textiles that the designer buys whenever she travels, journeys that

PRECEDING PAGE **In Tricia Guild's sitting room, a bench by Mauro Mori and a sofa and chair covered in Designers Guild fabric; the white lamp in the foreground is by Marcel Wanders for Cappellini. All of the furniture, fabrics, and accessories are from the Designers Guild shop in London.**

OPPOSITE **At the far end of the sitting room, a chair and cocktail table designed by Antonio Citterio; the sofa is upholstered in Rovego fabric by Designers Guild.**

design details

- mix textures in a room. I love the interplay of rich velvets, embroidered wools and cotton, and sturdy mohair
- windows dressed in fabric add interest to a room, but try using gauzy sheers and transparent silks combined with more substantial fabrics instead of heavy, lined curtains
- I prefer white ceilings and neutral-toned floors of painted white wood or stone tile or covered in a natural material such as sea-grass matting
- slipcover your upholstery for a refreshing seasonal change: I love the surprise of a summery large-scale floral linen over a quiet, solid-colored wool sofa
- choose a color palette that inspires you; gather fabric and paint swatches and photos of favorite interiors, divide them into color groups, and experiment with those that please you most
- don't be too timid with color; just maintain a good balance between whites and neutrals and more intense hues
- refine your tastes and know what you can and can't live with. I find shades of blue very restful and could never sleep in a yellow bedroom

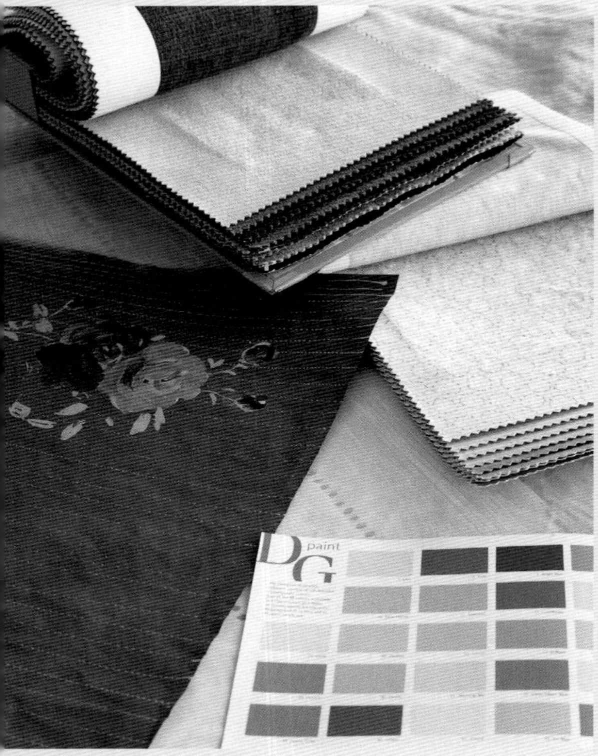

are as much research trips as they are vacations.

"I suppose I love to travel because I find things I can't find anywhere else. It's slightly alarming to find the same thing all over, on Madison Avenue and the Via Condotti and Sloane Street," says Guild. "I love finding beautiful things to look at." She is happiest traveling through India, which has been a source of joy throughout her career. "It's completely inspiring to me: the soul, the spirit, the tradition, the architecture."

The colors that Guild lives and works with have an Indian flamboyance, though she is energized by Sweden, Bali, Malaysia, and points beyond as well. But more important than the colors is the way Guild uses them to express her philosophy of design: design is a statement of individuality. Paint is rubbed roughly on the walls, for instance, instead of applied in a perfectly smooth, all-over coat. In her bathroom, towels are hung in alternating layers of purple and white. And in her walk-in closet, clothes are hung against shelves and rods painted bold chartreuse. It is a no-boundaries mentality that has made Guild's haute-hippie exuberance an infectious addition to the design landscape.

The Kings Road store is a direct reflection of Guild's intensely personal style. "The store has heart, people get it," she says. "Some things are Designers Guild, many are not. I don't want everything to be madly precious and one-off pieces. Good, honest things—furniture, tableware, fabrics, books, a great cup of coffee, or a wonderful olive oil—I love that concept. It's fantastic when I walk down the street and see curtains and they're made of our fabric; it's very exciting when someone's touched by what you do."

OPPOSITE **Guild and her restaurateur husband entertain frequently. Their guests often join them in their open-plan kitchen with its center island. The wall is paved in marine-blue tile; the counters are stainless steel, the cabinetry galvanized metal.**

RIVER
CAFE
COOK
BOOK
TWO
Pivotelli
ORSO

ellen o’

Ellen O'Neill likes themes, which is hardly surprising. As group vice-president of home design for Polo Ralph Lauren, she heads a team that realizes Ralph Lauren Home's themed lifestyle visions, from urban penthouse to Irish cottage. Recently, she decided it was time her rambling apartment—located a few blocks from Central Park in the Carnegie Hill area of Manhattan—had a new look, too. "Every night, outside my windows I see this skyline with black buildings and twinkling white lights, and I just took that as my direction," says O'Neill. "I wanted to create a tongue-in-cheek, black-and-white salute to a New York City environment.

"This place had always been like a Swedish fairy tale, very calming, with lots of Carl Larsson pastels and pale furniture," O'Neill says, referring to the turn-of-the-century Scandinavian artist and illustrator

neill

who launched a particularly Nordic brand of humble, homespun chic. But when she bought a house in the historic whaling village of Sag Harbor, at the eastern end of Long Island, "I realized that look really belonged out there. Then my daughter, Bridget, went away to college, and I was ready for a change. I knew I could graduate from the naïve and acknowledge the fact that I was living in an urban landscape."

Curiously, although the apartment's longtime decor had a soft, sweet attitude, "I've always had an orientation towards black and white—anything that's typewritten or with a message—flashcards, newsprint," says O'Neill, whose daily uniform is typically head-to-toe black and white. "I'm drawn to things that are straightforward and functional, things that are honest and humble. Black and white is constant and timeless and classic and never looks like you tried too hard."

So, it was back to the aesthetic drawing board. O'Neill began collecting black-and-white checked and striped fabrics, including wide awning-striped cotton from Provence. "It's funny, all of a sudden, everything just appeared," she says. "Once your eye is trained to something, it reveals itself, and everywhere you go, you latch onto more of it."

Perfection, however, it wasn't. Not at first. "All this was too edgy and radical for me," she says of the apartment's changing look. "I cleaned up and cleared out bags of things I'd accumulated. I gave things away and sold all my old furniture. And I sat there, thinking I was supposed to be thoroughly hip and modern and cool, divested of all my stuff, and it was like I was in a hospital. I *hated* it. There wasn't anything of me around; I was trying to be something I wasn't."

However, once O'Neill started to add texture—woven baskets and sisal carpet, leopard-pattern wallpaper in the dining room, checked paper in the hall, the quirky scenic wallpaper in the entry—the space

PRECEDING PAGES **From left, Ellen O'Neill found the folding chairs at a barn sale; she was told they were used as portable seating for school sports events. Originally covered in Naugahyde, she reupholstered them in cotton canvas. Framed outtakes of Audrey Hepburn in "Funny Face" hang above. O'Neill and Peter, a mixed-breed adoptee, in the front hall, which is papered in cartoon-like sketches of Parisian scenes.**

OPPOSITE **The living-room sofa is slipcovered in a black-and-white striped cotton by Ralph Lauren Home. O'Neill fashioned the cocktail table from a horsehair trunk and cigar boxes.**

FOLLOWING PAGES **French doors lead from the living room to the dining room. The leopard wallpaper is by Ralph Lauren Home, the folding chairs are from IKEA.**

WIFE DRESSING BY ANNE FOGARTY
DIANA VREELAND
OUR LIVES IN PARIS
Houses
THE LION'S SHARE
LYTTON STRACHEY
CARRINGTON
A.L. KENNEDY
PARTYTIME
EL PRODUC

"Design is all about really living

in rooms"

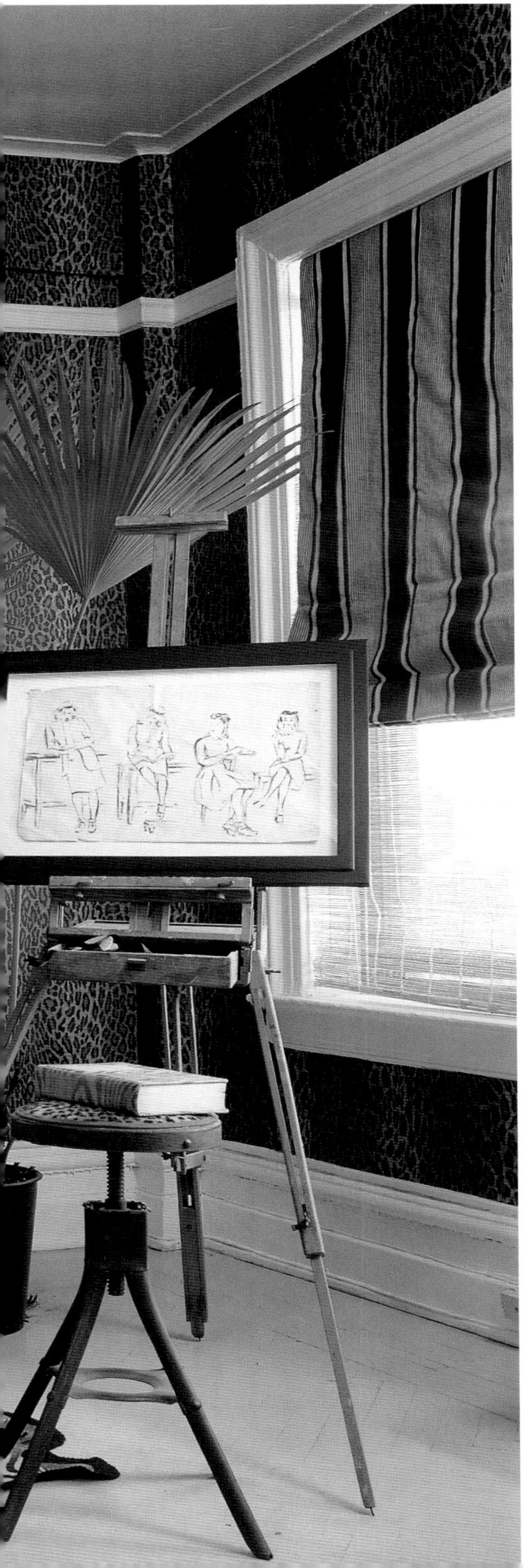

design details

- farmers' markets and food markets are great sources of inspiration for color and display
- it might sound crazy, but I like fabric and wallpaper to look faded and worn. I sometimes bleach fabric before I upholster or slipcover with it, or use it with the wrong side out
- I like to paint a white glaze over wallpaper that looks too bright, or I put tea in a spray bottle and spray the walls
- I live with pets and keep a lint brush in every room
- when I'm traveling, I always pay attention to the shopping bags that interesting-looking people are carrying; it's a good indication of which stores to check out
- I love flea markets, yard sales, estate sales
- I like to elevate the humble; don't be shy about framing and displaying a collection. Something as simple as vintage button cards from the '30s can be framed and hung on the wall as artwork
- I never take myself too seriously, and don't want to live with anything too precious

home office
THE RIGHT KIT AT THE RIGHT PRICE
30 THINGS YOU CAN'T WORK WITHOUT
ESSENTIALS FOR THE EFFICIENT HOME OFFICE

Muriel Brandolini's life has been an international whirlwind. The daughter of a French-Venezuelan mother and Vietnamese father, the designer ricocheted from a Saigon childhood, a Caribbean adolescence, and a Parisian education to a fast-paced career as a fashion stylist. Her latest incarnation is just as action-packed: celebrated decorator, wife of Italian-born banker Nuno Brandolini d'Adda, and mother of two young children.

The high-voltage Brandolini lifestyle is rich in inspiration. Frequent travel to far-flung destinations as well as a wide circle of intriguing and creative friends, family, and clients impel the designer to seek out the unusual and unexpected. She's inspired, too, by the magical interiors that the great Italian set designer and decorator Renzo Mongiardino created for her style-icon mother-in-law, Cristina, Countess Brandolino Brandolini d'Adda.

muriel b

randolini

As a result, Muriel Brandolini's imaginative and intricately detailed rooms are infused with a well-defined sense of drama and an endearing element of Auntie Mame-like whimsy.

"When I first started out," Brandolini says, "it was always about color: colorful fabrics, colorful walls." When the owner of a Manhattan apartment she used to sublet vetoed her proposal to paint his walls in a color more to her liking, she boldly curtained the premises, floor to ceiling, in panels of vivid fabrics. In one year, eleven international magazines had photographed the apartment, launching her design career and earning Brandolini a reputation for hippie chic, even though, she insists, "I'm not a hippie!"

Brandolini has a mind of her own and pays little attention to what other decorators are doing. She is known for being opinionated, blunt, demanding, and fast. "If the work can't be completed quickly, say, in six months, I lose the image and feel of what I wanted to do," she says. "I work from my gut—everything has to be fresh in my mind. Why waste time? I'm already on to the next project."

The decoration of her family's present home—an understated Victorian townhouse on a quiet, tree-lined block on Manhattan's Upper East Side—was completed at the usual lightning pace and hasn't been altered in five years. Behind its mousy brown façade is a tempest of color, energy, ornament, and exoticism. The entry opens onto a regal staircase and a sophisticated drawing room tucked at the rear of the house, its tables packed with opulent orchids. Not far away, however, Brandolini's office/study lies in a state of constant chaos. Walls are lined with design books, family photographs, and artwork by her children, Filippa and Brando. Samples of luxurious silks and stacks of Brandolini's rustic hand-blocked printed cottons

PRECEDING PAGE **Tufted love seats flank the drawing-room fireplace. The mixed-media painting is by Donald Baechler; the orchid cachepots are Vietnamese.**

OPPOSITE **A fire-engine red Chinese opium bed adds drama to the dining room; the portrait is of Count Nuno Brandolini, Muriel's husband, as a young boy. The walls and lampshades are covered in the designer's signature block-printed Indian fabrics.**

"I work from my gut—everything
mind. Why waste time? I'm alrea

has to be fresh in my
dy on to the next project"

LEFT **Brandolini painted the drawing room a watery blue-green and draped the doorway in a Chinese silk tapestry. She juxtaposed a Ross Bleckner painting, an Allegra Hicks carpet, a purple velvet sofa, and embroidered slipper chairs of her own design with a black-lacquer cocktail table from Madeleine Castaing in Paris.**

are scattered on the refectory table-cum-desk.

Entertaining well takes precedence chez les Brandolinis, and the more surprising, the better: the Christmas dinner menu, for example, is invariably classic Vietnamese cuisine. Downstairs is a large open kitchen, and nearby is the dining room, a cool fuchsia space dominated by a red-lacquer Chinese opium bed. The rectangular dining table is pulled alongside a twelve-foot-long leopard-print banquette (a gift from Brandolini's mother-in-law) and surrounded by an army of chairs with red velvet seats. Outside is a surprisingly tranquil bamboo garden.

In the deep coral master bedroom, Brandolini installed a Venetian chandelier, seventeenth-century side chairs, and an eccentric painted armoire designed by the Manhattan antiques dealer-designer R. Louis Bofferding. An adjacent library doubles as a screening room: books share shelf space with rows of classic film videos, and the screen descends from the ceiling, which is upholstered in a crazy-quilt of sparkling Indian and Asian fabrics. On the top floor, the children's bedroom doubles as a playroom, with the help of a Brandolini-designed playhouse/bunk bed complete with picket fence.

"I like a new challenge with each project," says the designer, who adheres to no rules and has no formula for success. "I don't have a living-room recipe or a bedroom recipe, an easy solution to do again and again. I like to surprise myself; it always has to be new."

Her work is clearly personality-driven, but she acknowledges the role the client plays in the whole process. "Yes, you can see it's my work," she says. "But I'm influenced by my clients and what they want. My interiors reflect them and their needs; they have to be lived in. Everything is not set in place and static: no one will ever say 'I can't move that bowl one inch because Muriel, my decorator, put it there!'"

OPPOSITE **In the master bedroom, an eighteenth-century carpet, a painted armoire, and a seventeenth-century side chair; the chandelier is Venetian.**

FOLLOWING PAGES **Clockwise from top left: Brando and Filippa's playhouse/bunk bed. Family photography and artwork line the shelves in Brandolini's office. A Brandolini lampshade in the drawing room.**

design details

- use color fearlessly. Have confidence in your choices, even if others don't
- scatter tabletops with funky, surefire eye-catchers found in nature, like coral branches (real or fake) and seashells
- group several pots of orchids together for a strong impact
- add pattern and color to a room by using painterly flat-weave carpets and exotic printed fabrics as curtains or upholstery. I often slipcover furniture in a patchwork of vintage fabrics
- to keep things lively, mix textures and finishes. I love the contrast of Madeleine Castaing's black-lacquer tables in a room layered in fabric
- never underestimate the power of good-quality artwork, even simple ceramics and glass
- don't take yourself too seriously—a sense of humor in decoration goes a long way

bijoux art déco
GRAPHICAR
Christian Dior
VANITAS
VERSACE
FORTUNY
VOGUE
ALLURE
DIANA VREELAND
CALDER'S UNIVERSE
PRIMITIVISM IN 20TH CENTURY ART
ROY LICHTENSTEIN
EROTIC POSTCARDS
BODYWATCHING
PALACES OF VENICE
THE HAMPTONS
PICASSO
WAR YEARS
ENGLISH FURNITURE
THE ELEGANT JAPANESE HOUSE
BEATON IN VOGUE
LE SIEGE FRANCAIS
THE BED AND BATH BOOK
MARRAKECH
PIERRE CHAREAU

catherine

Catherine Memmi understands luxury. With a sure, firm hand the Paris-based designer-retailing entrepreneur has created a mini home-furnishings empire with global impact. Her formula for success focuses on the use of rich, natural materials, monochromatic color, and the timeless appeal of cotton, linen, wool, and cashmere. Even casual passersby to her chic eponymous boutique in Saint-Germain-des-Près gets a sense of the seductive Memmi lifestyle: the air is fragrant and walls are lined with chocolate-brown wooden shelves stocked with soft towels, crisp bed linens, loose, sensual clothing, and beautifully designed tableware.

The Memmi color palette, limited to white, black, sand, brown, navy, and gray, has an occasional pale earthy shade thrown in for good measure. Her smartly packaged bath and beauty products, Les Basiques, are carefully

memmi

formulated and softly scented; her home-fragrance collection is subtle and never overpowers. This arbiter of understated elegance is also business-savvy: her fourteen boutiques are now located in five countries and her furniture and accessory designs and collections of bed and bath linens, home fragrance, and Les Basiques products are exported around the world.

Memmi's home is equally inspiring although a far more dramatic and powerful design statement in stark black and white. In a nineteenth-century building not far from her shops on the Left Bank, Memmi lives with her husband—CFO of the company—and sons in a spacious apartment laden with elaborate architectural detail. "This apartment reconciles two radically different tendencies—incredible nineteenth-century Parisian style and highly contemporary graphic symmetry. I like walking that fine line, balancing modern design and classicism."

The designer has carved out a clever floor plan, with public rooms on one side of the space and a long hall on the opposite side of the apartment, which leads to a private wing of bedrooms and baths. The main rooms, including a family-oriented petit salon, more formal grand salon, and a dining room-cum-home office are furnished with the clean silhouettes of sofas and chairs from her upholstery collections. All are covered in bright white cotton canvas, punctuated with cushions and throws in black or charcoal. The tables have simple lines and subtle finishes; lighting and accessories are spare as well, fashioned in nickel, chrome, or painted white.

Memmi's minimalist, modern furnishings are in sharp contrast to the apartment's beautifully preserved original moldings. The window

PRECEDING PAGE **In the grand salon of her Left Bank apartment, Catherine Memmi's Rue de Tournon sofa, Saint-Germain armchairs, and Week-end cocktail table.**

OPPOSITE **Linear, pared-down moldings frame the doors leading to the grand salon; they complement Memmi's modern furnishings and provide a sharp contrast to the formal nineteenth-century molding on the walls and ceiling in the next room. The Zen console tables and white lamps are Memmi designs.**

FOLLOWING PAGES **Clockwise from left, the dining room doubles as an ultra-chic home office; it is furnished with Memmi's Week-end dining table and Studio chairs. Hilton McConnico's *Reflecting Shadows* is displayed above Memmi's Manhattan wenge-wood console and nickel Zen lamps. Calla lilies and a Jean Cocteau drawing.**

treatments are understated as well, the casement windows are left bare or hung with tabbed cotton curtains hanging straight to the floor. Accordingly, the space is filled with sunlight, which only heightens the juxtaposition of modern and traditional by accentuating the chalky white swags and flourishes on the walls and ceilings.

Although as pared-down as it can be, the apartment is far from cold: the petit salon has floor-to-ceiling shelves casually piled with books, magazines, and photographs, and the Memmi boys have free run of the rooms. The family also has a farmhouse in Normandy, where a bit more texture and clutter have crept in, but in Paris, Memmi says, "I wanted a strong feeling of serenity and comfort; this is a place for creative thinking and rest."

OPPOSITE AND LEFT **Memmi designed the spacious kitchen, which pairs stainless-steel efficiency with charming casement windows and a floor tiled in classic black and white.**

FOLLOWING PAGES **Clockwise from top left, the luxe brown and beige master bedroom: the Zen bed, pinstripe sheets, merino-wool blanket, and chrome New York lamps are by Memmi. A wardrobe on wheels and a Tokyo chair in the dressing room. The clothing in cotton, linen, wool, and cashmere was designed by Memmi. The bath is sheathed in white marble; the bath and beauty products are from Memmi's Les Basiques line.**

DAVID HICKS
LIVING WITH DESIGN
EDWARD RUSCHA
EDITIONS 1959–1999
LOST HOLLYWOOD
FILM GUIDE
SPAIN

kathryn

"I think I do houses that have soul, that look lived in," says interior designer Kathryn Ireland. "The best compliment I've ever had about a house I'd done is that it didn't look a bit like a decorator had been there. I was absolutely delighted." Clearly, Ireland isn't someone who takes herself—or her profession—too seriously. In fact, she says, "'Serious' is a word you want to completely avoid when it comes to decorating."

British-born and Los Angeles-based, Ireland has lived in the States for fifteen years. Having raced through a variety of careers—public relations, fashion, acting, and styling and producing music videos—she finally found her true aesthetic calling. In 1990, she and the actress Amanda Pays opened Ireland-Pays, a chic closet of a home-furnishings store in Santa Monica, where they sold "all the bits that make a house look like a home"—

ireland

vintage fabrics and tableware, cushions, baskets, and lamps. Ireland later expanded to a larger eponymous shop on Montana Avenue and took on full-fledged design projects. She sold home accessories, furniture, and her signature line of printed-hemp fabrics there until recently, when she closed the shop to concentrate on her design studio. Her fabrics are now available in several shops and showrooms, including Hollyhock Hilldale in Los Angeles and John Rosselli in Manhattan.

It's a happy, hectic life, populated by three young sons—Oscar, Otis, and Louis—small, frantic, scurrying dogs, and the burgeoning business. During the summer months, the Ireland clan decamps to a farmhouse in the south of France, "where it's all about family, countryside, horses, fruit trees, and chickens," she says. "I think you lose something when you work all the time. My time there with my family really informs my creativity, and I'm up-front with new clients that I'll communicate with my office by fax, but I *will* be away."

Clients like Caroline Kennedy Schlossberg, Steve Martin, Lorne Michaels, and Lady Annabel Goldsmith don't seem to mind. They're drawn to Ireland's casual, spirited take on design, best exemplified by her own digs, a 1920s house whose Spanish-style architecture is typical of the Santa Monica area. Unpretentious and friendly, it's all rustic white walls, wooden beams, arched doorways, and comfortable furniture. The drawing room has a vaulted ceiling, the dining room opens onto a trellised terrace and spacious yard, the kitchen is warmed by handmade Mexican tile, and the family room and bedrooms are accented with Ireland's French-inspired fabrics.

Spontaneity is key: Jack Russell terriers march on the sofa cushions, the designer's sons have the run of the place, and crowds of friends materialize for impromptu dinner parties. Ireland's style is relaxed yet

PRECEDING PAGES **Kathryn Ireland hung a collection of seventeenth-century engravings of Jesuit priests—purchased in an English countryside junk shop for a mere five pounds—above the arched doorway in her drawing room.**

OPPOSITE **In the drawing room, an early eighteenth-century commode with intricate marquetry inlay; the seventeenth-century Italian mirror is one of Ireland's favorite pieces.**

““Serious’ is a word you want to avoid when

completely
it comes to decorating"

LEFT **The drawing room features an inviting mix of classic, neutral-toned upholstery and assorted cushions covered in a dizzying array of fabrics. The over-mantel mirror is flanked by acanthus candleholders.**

chic, her decor is stylish yet pragmatic; her environment is all about rooms that make sense. "I think people find it hard to pull things together without it looking too contrived," she says. "They come to me because they want a little bit of clutter. Warmth and clutter—that I can do."

OPPOSITE AND LEFT **The kitchen and family room open onto a terrace shaded by a vine-covered pergola; Ireland intersperses woven armchairs from Italy with wooden side chairs. The rustic pine cupboard in the kitchen displays photos of the decorator's sons—Oscar, Otis, and Louis—pottery, and cookbooks.**

FOLLOWING PAGES **Clockwise from top left, a detail of the master bedroom, which features a half-tester bed hung with fringed crewelwork curtains. The family-room curtains are made from a signature patchwork of her French-influenced printed hemp fabrics. The guest room is decorated in Ireland's pale-green prints.**

design details

- if you go simple, you can't go wrong
- I love comfort: sofas should be big, deep, and soft
- it's hard to make a room feel warm and lived in if everything in it is new: the finish is so important on a new piece of furniture and mixing in antiques is always best
- I design rooms as if I'd be living there
- I have to be able to laugh with my clients; curtain fabric is just not worth fighting over
- I like rooms where everything has a purpose: there are chairs by the fire, a good sofa, a proper cocktail table
- my favorite colors are sort of 'off' colors—apple green, maize yellow, brick red
- if you go big, you take away the preciousness of something: I much prefer to do a last-minute dinner for twenty than a planned little supper for four
- simple things are luxuries to me: nice taps, good doorknobs, terrific pillows. Detail is luxury
- I'd rather buy less and make sure it is good
- there's no rule that you have to decorate all at once if you can't afford it. Just do one great room at a time

liz o'b

rien

Liz O'Brien is known for her intellectual, scholarly approach to design, but her home—a large loft above her former shop in downtown Manhattan—is an anything-but-staid mix of exuberant color and striking decoration. A leading dealer of twentieth-century decorative arts, O'Brien operates an eponymous gallery—now located on Fifth Avenue in midtown Manhattan—specializing in furniture masters of the 1940s, '50s and '60s, such as T. H. Robsjohn-Gibbings, Tommi Parzinger, Jean-Michel Frank, Billy Haines, and Samuel Marx. Not surprisingly, several of their designs made their way upstairs. "Some of this furniture was originally in my shop and didn't attract a lot of attention," O'Brien says. "I would think, 'this is far too good to not be noticed; I'll just take it home.'"

Although designers such as Ray and Charles Eames and George Nelson dominated the postwar era, using new materials and techniques to

"I don't really need to keep

things; I like to find things"

PRECEDING PAGES **Clockwise from far left, a drawing by Lucio Fontana, ceramics by Gambone, and a limed-oak bookcase Samuel Marx designed for his own house. Liz O'Brien in her eponymous Manhattan shop. In O'Brien's living room, wrought-iron and limed oak bookshelves found at a Paris flea market, a ceramic deer head by Jean-René Gauguin, 1940s mirror by Line Vautrin, Samuel Marx armchairs, and a slipper chair by Billy Haines.**

LEFT **In the living room, a sofa and armchair by Samuel Marx and ceramic lamps by Cecile Coverly on side tables by Edward Wormley for Dunbar. The painting is by David Roth, the cocktail table is by Tommi Parzinger, the V'Soske rug is circa 1939, and the patinated-metal sculpture is by Tony Duquette.**

create mass-market, inexpensive pieces, O'Brien is drawn to luxe designs commissioned by a far more exclusive clientele. She collects and deals in the rarified, beautifully detailed furniture and accessories made for urbane, socially prominent clients who sought the only best in craftsmanship and quality. "It doesn't have to be grand or expensive," she insists. "I actually like very humble, charming things. Even though the furniture and accessories I deal in are very high-style, they do show a lot of 'hand.'"

Despite the heady provenance of its furnishings, her loft is a bit playful and surprisingly livable. Decorator Muriel Brandolini, a client, consulted with O'Brien on the paint colors and had a strong influence on the apartment's fabrics and furniture placement. "Muriel is both opinionated and fast, and she picked these wildly intense colors in about five minutes," O'Brien says. "I would have vacillated for months. But not only would this furniture have been lost in a white apartment, this space is dark and the architecture is hardly extraordinary; it's a perfect place to experiment with color."

In the Chinese-red living room, subtly textured, neutral-toned upholstered furniture stands out sharply against the color-punched walls. O'Brien mixed a Marx sofa, slipper chairs by Haines, a pewter-topped, carved-wood cocktail table by Parzinger, and a prized circa-1939 V'Soske rug. Chests and bookcases by Marx and side tables by Edward Wormley support a plethora of wittily chic accessories: Cecile Coverly lamps, a patinated-metal sculpture by designer Tony Duquette, a 1940s mirror by French jewelry designer Line Vautrin, vintage photographs, and Italian ceramics and drawings.

The dining room, which is painted an Yves Saint Laurent-style fuchsia, is centered around a lacquered-wood Parzinger table inlaid

with a grid motif. From the ceiling, with its baroque painted decoration, hangs a candle-powered chandelier by Baguès, a French metalwork firm that famously created lighting for everyone from English decorator Syrie Maugham to the Duchess of Windsor. "Everything in this place had to have soul and originality," says O'Brien.

Dealers can be pack rats, but "I'm not like that," O'Brien swears. "I don't really need to keep things, I like to find things. I find something, learn everything about it, and then can let it go. All along, I've had this great idea that if you clear the way, if you let go of one thing, another great thing will come. Sometimes, I'll sell something, only to think, 'Oh my God, I'll never have one like that again!' But if a fabulous chandelier goes out the door, a great carpet comes in the next day. Now that's what I find exciting."

ABOVE **In the dining room, a Tommi Parzinger lacquered-wood table, parchment chest by Samuel Marx, Venetian-glass lamp, folding chairs by Jansen, and a Baguès tole chandelier decorated with a crystal garland.**

FOLLOWING PAGES **From left, Casablanca lilies and rock-crystal votives. A shop display of Line Vautrin mirrors. A baroque frieze painted on the dining-room ceiling. Samuel Marx designed both the Queen Anne-style lacquer chair and the Lucite-and-lacquer side table; the textile is Indian silk.**

design details

- don't use overhead lighting or track lighting. Lamplight is best, or use cove lighting or spotlights
- don't allow yourself to live without art. I especially love drawings and works on paper, which are surprisingly affordable
- basics, like tennis shoes, should be white. White bed linens and white towels keep my choices simple; I'd rather focus on more important things
- don't compromise: furniture should always be comfortable
- candles in grassy, natural scents such as Diptyque's Mousse, Lierre, and Foin Coupe are so subtle, you can burn them all day
- I always have music playing—from classical to samba to jazz to soundtracks. I enjoy listening to classical radio stations; I learn about music that I wouldn't otherwise think to buy
- don't be afraid to use humble flowers—hydrangeas, marigolds, anemones, and amaryllis. They contrast well with almost any style of furniture and accessories

celia

"Our neighbors used to call this the 'Addams Family' house," says Celia Tejada, describing her lovingly restored 1890s Victorian, situated on a hilly street near San Francisco's Golden Gate Park. A former fashion designer, now vice-president of product design for Pottery Barn, Tejada renovated the wreck of a house with her contractor brother Ivo. Home to her, her young sons Aristos and Tristan, Ivo, and her mother, the house seems to have taken on a life and personality of its own, and continues to evolve, a creative work in progress.

Tejada was living in a minimalist modern apartment when her brother learned the Victorian relic was for sale. "He called to tell me he found the house of my dreams," she says. "Although walls were falling down and it hadn't been painted in thirty years, it was a fabulous building; it had great bones. I said I would buy it

tejada

So long as a woman has twinkles in her eyes, no man notices whether she has wrinkles under them.
— Dolores Del Rio
Picture
SMILE

Menú
Flan

only on the condition that Ivo would renovate it with me. And so he did."

The lacy, white Victorian exterior gives no hint of the energy and color that exist within. Tejada remodeled room by room, creating unique spaces that are highly personal and extremely practical. Steep stairs lead to a cozy entry and nearby "image room"—a warm yellow parlor hung with a collage of framed photographs, words, and phrases that have meaning for her and her family. Just as striking as the room-as-album idea is the owner's sense of fun: tiny photos are embraced by oversize mattes, baby photos have been printed to larger-than-life scale. "I wanted to have a gallery of images of my life," Tejada says. "These are my roots, my dreams; they're inspiration pictures." Born and raised in Ruerrero, a small village in northern Spain, Tejada is the lone daughter in a family of five sons. Family is of paramount importance to her. "This room is very much about this house and the lives of the people who live here."

The space also serves as the media room. A projection screen descends from the ceiling, velvet blackout curtains close, and the family lounges on an immense sofa layered with faux-fur throws and soft cushions. It's a communal approach that Tejada finds particularly suited to her extended family's life under one roof. "I don't particularly like the idea of watching TV, but if I can make watching TV or a movie a family affair, it becomes more special, something we can share."

The dining room plays host to Sunday-evening dinner parties, which are often themed. The iron chandelier is usually decorated—like an airborne centerpiece—and the menu and guests are listed on blackboards. Down the hall, the open kitchen is sunny and spacious. "Entertaining is so important to me," Tejada says, "and I put a lot of thought into the kitchen area. I'm only five-feet tall and I didn't want

PRECEDING PAGE **In the "image room" of her San Francisco Victorian, Celia Tejada arranged graphic framed words and photographs. The room also features a projection television/movie screen that descends from the ceiling, velvet blackout curtains, and a deep, seventeen-foot-long sofa with fifty-eight cushions.**

OPPOSITE **Tejada found the iron dining-room chandelier at a country store in Sonoma and added strands of crystal beads. At her ritual Sunday-evening dinner parties, Tejada lists the menu, guests, and theme of the evening on the blackboards displayed over the sideboard, which was built by her brother Ivo.**

to be overwhelmed by cabinets. We built a fabulous pantry and all the other storage is under-counter. I installed a big stove where I can cook my favorite paella, and we created the 'siesta room,' so Aristos and Tristan can read or take a nap nearby."

This area, a niche with a wall-to-wall mattress and a dozen pillows, is in an atrium-like end of the kitchen, which opens onto a terrace with a gurgling tiled fountain. Here, it's clear Tejada has kept the Victorian essence of this house and added a healthy dollop of Mediterranean flavor. "Victorians tend to be a little finicky," she says. "I wanted this house to have more heart."

Upstairs, Ivo's suite is painted a rich suede-brown. Their mother's bedroom, a soft blue, boasts an iron bed and a claw-foot bathtub set in front of the bay window. The guest room, a study in black and white, features a bed canopied in white linen. In place of a headboard, Tejada stenciled a stretched canvas with a simple admonishment that is also her favorite word: "Dream."

Aristos and Tristan share a bedroom painted tomato red; their bath has a small sink set into the wall at little-boy height. "This was inexpensive and easy to do and makes the boys feel like the house is for them," Tejada says. Upstairs, she created a duplex suite for herself: a bedroom and bath on separate floors that run the length of the attic. Her large bathtub is set in the middle of the bathroom under an enormous skylight. "At the end of the day, your house should be your private world," she says. "At night, I draw a bath, turn off the lights, set out the candles, and watch the stars. This is what I once only dreamed of; it's magical."

OPPOSITE **The kitchen features under-counter cabinets, a commercial-style stove, flea-market lighting, and a stainless-steel island and stools from a restaurant-supply store.**

FOLLOWING PAGES **From left, favorite photos and objects in the second-floor office. Tejada clips pictures and notes to a clothesline suspended over the desk by pulleys. Collections of watches, clocks, and cameras are artfully displayed.**

¿A qué huelen los sueños?
king is like love, it should be enterentered into with abandon or not at all

design details

- the things that people seem to enjoy most about my house are the unusual things—the screening room, the children's sink—that are so easy to do, and that make it a much more personal space
- I collect pulleys—like clothesline pulleys—that I find in flea markets and hardware stores. I use them all over the house, even the chandeliers hang from them so they can be lowered to light the candles. The one over the boys' bathtub holds a basket of their toys; after a bath, I just hoist it up out of the way and the toys drip dry. It's a funny way to make life easier
- each bedroom has a faux-fur throw; you can never be too cozy
- if you keep your collections in well-organized displays, they have more clarity
- I also collect letters: wooden letters, plaster letters, and letters from signs and printing shops. I arrange them in different places and my family and friends redo them. I've also hung chalkboards in almost every room. Everyone wants to scribble and draw on them
- painting the bedrooms different colors has allowed the people who live here to create their own territories
- I like simple white tableware that allows the food to be the star. Great wine and food, and how you dress the table—that's what makes a real evening
- my life is a mix of my values from my small village in Spain and the social integrity and efficiency of the States; here, everything is possible!

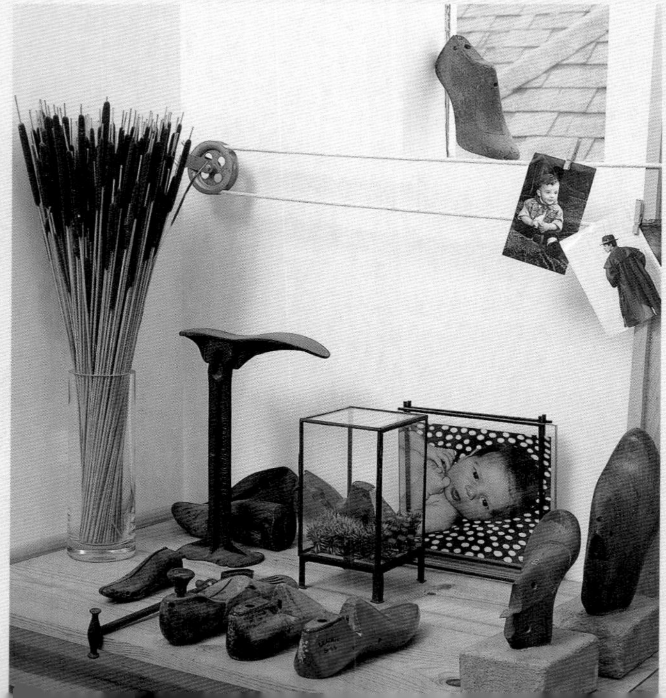

FLASH
REDIAL
WARNER BOOKS
Elements of Style Phillip Bloch

DREAM
WAR OFFICE 1886 1892

OPPOSITE AND ABOVE **Tejada's favorite word is stenciled on canvas above the guest-room bed, which is draped in yards of white linen. A bedside table in Tejada's attic bedroom, which runs the length of the house.**

FOLLOWING PAGES **Clockwise from left, Tejada with sons Tristan, left, and Aristos, right, in the boys' tomato-red bedroom. The "siesta room," just off the kitchen, is a niche with a king-size, cushion-covered daybed, perfect for reading or napping. The children's bath features a small sink installed at child-friendly height.**

"Victorians tend to be a little finicky.
house to have more heart"

wanted this

sheila

bridges

"I try to help my clients understand that good design and great style are accessible," Manhattan-based designer Sheila Bridges says, "that style isn't just something you see in books and magazines." Her eight-room apartment, located in a landmark 1901 building in Harlem, bears eloquent witness to this personal philosophy. It is rife with architectural detail—high ceilings, two fireplaces, and wainscoting. But it's how the space is furnished that has made it Bridges's calling card. "Clients see how I live and work here," she says. "There's a sense of home, of what I can help them create for themselves. This place isn't a series of rooms staged to look a certain way, it's testimony that my design works."

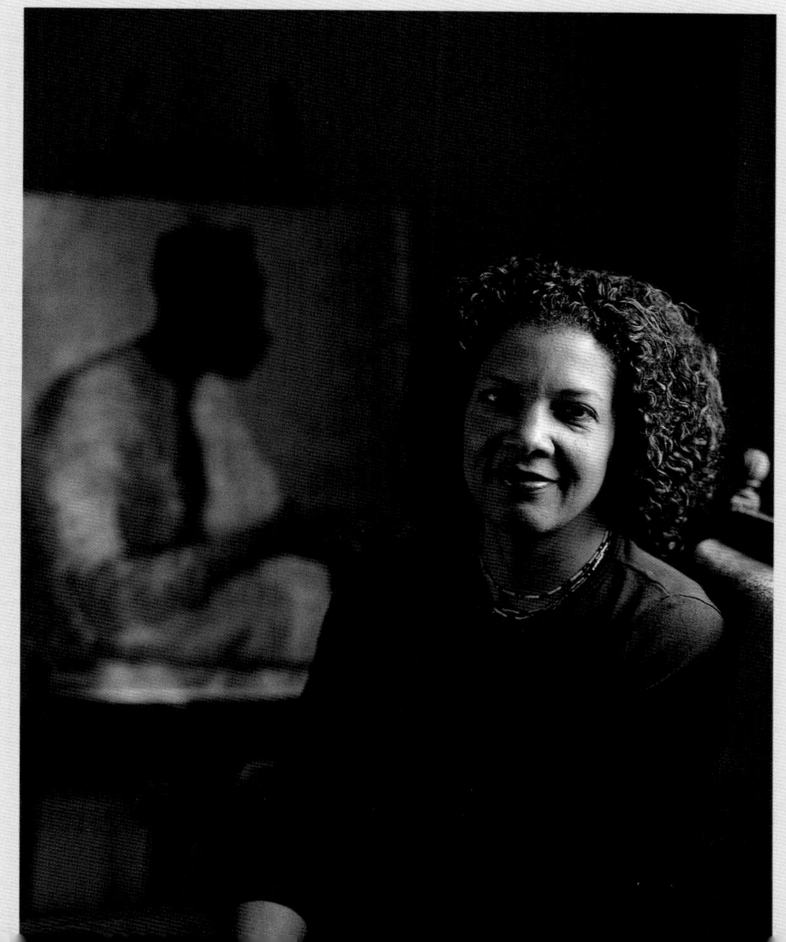

Bridges has created understated, modernist rooms that combine a homespun foundation with rich details and

PRECEDING PAGES **In her wainscoted living room, Sheila Bridges mixes neutral-toned cotton and linen upholstery, iron tables topped with granite or marble, sisal carpeting, and flea-market finds such as an armillary sphere and an amateur's take on Kandinsky on the far wall.**

OPPOSITE AND LEFT **The centerpiece of the moody, blue-green bedroom is an antique painted iron bed; Bridges likes the spirited juxtaposition of the *Easter Sunday/Harlem* photograph in an elaborate Victorian frame. The bathroom is a study in black and white: the medicine cabinet, which she painted black, is by Waterworks, as are the nickel sink fittings. The brass sconces were found in Paris.**

FOLLOWING PAGES **From left, a leaded-glass cabinet holds Depression glass and wedding crystal inherited from Bridges's grandmother. Parrot tulips in an etched-glass vase. Antique lyre-back chair with monogrammed silk pillows. The mantel and tile fireplace surround are original to the space; accessories range from decorative objects chosen to accent the room to family treasures.**

a practically papal sense of color. In her living room the upholstery is natural cotton and linen elevated by luxe touches delivered in small but choice doses: pillows of taffeta, an antique side chair covered in elegant Fortuny, tufted silk cushions on a pair of iron stools. It's a hint of formality in a not-very-formal place. The bedroom is a deep blue-green sanctuary while her bath is more startling, with dramatic black walls beneath a brilliant blue ceiling of polished Venetian-style plaster.

Underscoring it all is the designer's preference for classical form and her distaste for overly ornate furniture and objects, an approach that she developed in her years at the Parsons School of Design and a New York architectural office.

"When I started out, I wanted to create access to design for African-Americans," says Bridges. "What's important now is that it's all about good design and not about hiring somebody who is black."

design details

- I like to take a fresh look at classic things, to create rooms with resonance and a sense of history
- it's easier for clients to tell you what they don't like than what they do
- rooms and their furnishings shouldn't be too precious; you should be able to really live in them
- I'm drawn to objects that at first glance don't seem particularly special, but up close something sets them apart
- sisal and sea-grass are my favorite floor coverings: they suit any style of decor and are inexpensive. If linoleum was the surface of the '50s, and shag carpet that of the '60s, sisal is it for today
- I like accessories with personality, with a sense of meaning and tradition; they give a room its soul
- I take inspiration from the outdoors and try to bring natural, earthy colors inside

mariette

himes gomez

Once the parlor floor of a "private house of great distinction," Mariette Himes Gomez's pied-à-terre apartment overlooks Sloane Gardens, a leafy enclave in Chelsea, the epicenter of London life. The interiors, however, perfectly illustrate that Gomez is an American, first and foremost: crisp, tailored, rational, a place for everything, and everything in its place. But, the Michigan-born, Manhattan-based designer says, even though she ignored the expected—brocade curtains, period fireplace, and European pictures—"I don't think I was disrespectful to the fact that it is a flat in England."

For instance, though the neatness is thoroughly Yankee, the furniture and objects are largely homegrown: a Gothic-style step back cabinet, an Irish console table, a mahogany mirror from an old country house, a chair from a dealer friend near Brighton. Old-fashioned, yes, but not without a splash of comfortable modernity. The centerpiece of the drawing room is a 100-inch-long sofa designed and owned by Syrie Maugham, a celebrated Chelsea resident of the 1930s who created the kind of no-color rooms that are echoed in Gomez's own spaces. "It's too large for anywhere else in my life," she says. "But it's great here." The floor is swathed in sisal matting, another English style hallmark, but the drawing-room curtains are as far from classic flounces and furbelows as Gomez could get.

"I didn't want them encumbered by fabric," says the designer, who installed one of her trademarks: raw-silk curtains that operate as shutters, the fabric panels mounted on hinged rods that open into the room. "The idea of covering windows is so odd to me," she adds. "You're covering half the light, the trees, the buildings."

A survivor from the house's Victorian youth, the tracery ceiling of the drawing room shelters Gomez's personal take on an eighteenth-century print room. From floor to ceiling is a lively mosaic of framed art: architectural drawings, prints, watercolors, lithographs, charcoal drawings and photographs. "Some are even from my daughter's school," says the designer, who went into business for herself thirty years ago as a work-at-home mother, after cutting her teeth at the New York society decorators Parish-Hadley and the office of modernist architect Edward Durrell Stone. "I like that they have meaning to me." Keeping the eclectica under control was crucial: The frames are either gold, black or a mixture of both. "When you put that many pictures on a wall, there has to be some order."

And some surrounding calm, too. "I'm noted for very neutral

PRECEDING PAGES **In the drawing room, a pair of Italian painted armchairs and an Irish silver table. The sofa was designed by the 1930s English decorator Syrie Maugham, its original owner. In front of it, Gomez placed her atypical take on the prosaic cocktail table—an extra-long caned bench covered with a button-tufted squab, or thin cushion, made of old curtain fabric.**

OPPOSITE **The drawing room's ceiling is patterned with plaster tracery in the form of Moorish-style stars; the walls are covered in pale yellow embossed linen. Gomez rescued the modernist wood mantel from one of her showhouse rooms. The painted Gothic-style cabinet was purchased in the Kings Road.**

“I never wanted anything to

feel like a color scheme"

LEFT **Inspired by eighteenth-century print rooms, Gomez hung a collection of framed architectural and garden prints on the drawing-room walls; the mahogany doors are original. The circa-1820 mahogany mirror came from a large country house. The linen-upholstered armchairs were bought at a London decorative-arts fair.**

design details

- strive for comfort in the living room and convenience in the kitchen. Install the television in the library, and emphasize luxury in the bedroom and bath
- paint colors formulated by Donald Kaufman are beyond compare
- I like the color of a candle to complement its candlestick: vanilla candles in silver candlesticks, medium brown candles in copper, brass, or bronze, chocolate candles in wood, and ivory-colored candles in glass
- recycle antique textiles and beaded fabric fragments as cushion covers
- accessories in geometric shapes are interesting: squares, circles, cubes, spheres, or any polyhedrons
- I love old linen and vintage Wedgwood drabware
- symmetry anchors a room: use pairs of tables, chairs, bookcases, or any decorative objects

FRA FILIPPO LIPPI
The Carmelite Painter
MEGAN HOLMES

spaces," she says, almost apologetically, though she insists that she's as colorful as anyone else in her field, just more modulated in her approach. "Color is a subtlety to me. If I do have color, I want to have it a certain way, on the floor, in accessories and art, not the whole thing. I never wanted anything to feel like a color scheme." At home, she gravitates toward the tones that have made her reputation as a modernist with a luxurious edge—oatmeal, linen, cream, and ivory, spiked with polished mahogany and dressmaker fabrics like linen and silk. Even the small bedroom is swathed in tidily tailored cream-and-tan stripes that make the small room—which is "higher than it is

PRECEDING PAGES **Clockwise from bottom left, beautifully bound leather books. A tetrahedron and a silver cuff and candlestick are displayed on the mantel. Raw-silk curtains, on hinged rods, dress the floor-to-ceiling French doors. An Italian painted chair.**
OPPOSITE AND ABOVE **In the kitchen, a collection of export china, earthenware, and transferware on an antique plate rack. Trompe-l'oeil lace curtains and a whimsical egg border were painted on the cabinets.**

ABOVE **A French mirror and Gothic shelf in the hallway.**

OPPOSITE **Gomez used a pinstripe fabric by Gretchen Bellinger to make curtains and upholster her bedroom walls. The bed canopy and side curtains are recycled from one of the designer's showhouse rooms; mounted at the ceiling, their height makes the cozy room appear more spacious.**

wide"—seem larger than its proportions would indicate on a floor plan.

"It's the perfect spot to begin the day with tea and toast, which I would never take the time to do in New York. Over here, life is more leisurely. And everything in London is 'please' and 'thank you,' which helps make me remember to be a person first." Also, she says with a laugh, the time difference between Manhattan and Chelsea helps, "No one needs me back in the office until it's two in the afternoon here, so I might even get a chance to relax a bit before doing whatever needs to be done."

anita cal

ero

Colombian-born photographer Anita Calero lives in a home of compelling contrasts: a boxy white loft that gives the impression of being a rambling house, its aura of Zen-like calm constant despite the free rein of her canary and parrot—Pupalacho and Marybird—who chatter and chirp as they swoop and zoom throughout the rooms. Calero's space has presence: her spare decor is thoughtfully chosen, with a photographer's eye for memorable juxtapositions, and there is always sweet incense burning, music playing, an exotic flower tucked into a rustic vase. It is the home of someone with style and taste, someone about whom the French would say, "Elle est bien dans sa peau," that she is happy with herself.

Calero lives in what is now considered prime real estate: a 2,000-square-foot loft on an art gallery-dotted block in Manhattan's Chelsea district. But the neighborhood's cutting-edge, smart-set reputation is still relatively recent. When Calero found her future home, she was able to spot potential few would have been able to imagine.

She had searched for a new place for more than a year, hoping to find raw space that could accommodate a photo studio. The building she found, formerly a printing plant, was previously zoned for commercial use only. As for the loft, not only was it in a state of total disrepair, but there were large, explicitly erotic artworks in every corner: the previous resident, a sculptor, specialized in pornographic art. "You have *no* idea," Calero laughs. "But as soon as I walked in, I knew—even with all that—this was the place for me."

A gut renovation followed, though, at the time, she had only a long-term lease. (The building has since been sold and she purchased the apartment.) "My lawyer cautioned me about the cost," she says. "But the investment was a one-time expense that is a daily benefit—I love living in comfort, and what I added is very simple, very basic." A designer-friend helped divide the space into private and professional areas: the kitchen and master bedroom and bath are situated on one side of the open living/shooting area, and an office, library, guest room, and bath are on the other. After Calero finally closed on the loft, she decided she wanted it to be more of a private space and now rarely schedules photo shoots there. "It just became too intrusive," she says. "I couldn't believe it, clients would wander in to my bedroom and want to check out my closets. And I'm really a terribly private person." Her studio manager runs Calero's photography business out of the small office, but the main room—despite its scale—now seems less a photo studio and more a stylish living room.

PRECEDING PAGES **From left, a circa-1950 Jean Prouvé table and chairs in the kitchen. Anita Calero in her library; she designed the Brancusi-inspired bookshelves, handmade of sandblasted ash.**

OPPOSITE **In the entry to Calero's loft, a Maria Robledo photograph, vintage Serge Mouille table lamp, and a colorful stack of cubes—once used as a teaching aid—from the 1950s.**

FOLLOWING PAGES **From left, in the living area, a painting by James Brown, a pair of vintage sofas and a stool by mid-century furniture craftsman George Nakashima, and a 1950s Swedish table. The mustard-color linen wall hanging is an antique English bedcover.**

The apartment has three exposures and is filled with sun. "I like the light, it's what first attracted me," Calero says. "I kept the walls white because of the photography, but added a little color when I started shooting in other studios." The floors were stripped of carpet and layers of paint, revealing concrete that bears the earthy patina of years of commercial use. They complement Calero's furnishings—wooden and ceramic accessories, rustic antique textiles, and choice pieces by twentieth-century modernist masters such as Charlotte Perriand, George Nakashima, and Jean Royère—with warm finishes that have only grown richer with age.

Both utilitarian and chic, there is an elegant economy to Calero's kitchen. The dining table and chairs are vintage Prouvé. The under-counter

“I’m not into the ‘new thing.’ . . . The new thing for me is a classic thing”

dark wood cabinets open to reveal china and cookware in pristine order. Serving accessories and vases are lined up with careful precision on open shelves, and photos and mementos are displayed on a cork-faced Sub-Zero refrigerator. Calero, a former photo stylist, creates a day-to-day series of still lifes; there is a constant artful composition of fruit and vegetables on the windowsill. The bath features a rustic oak sink and brushed-chrome fittings; the walls are covered in white subway tile. "I'm not into the 'new thing,'" she says. "The new thing for me is a classic thing—it's simple, white tile; it's old silver; it's sleeping on vintage linen sheets from the Paris flea market. I don't just collect these things; I use them."

Though there is nothing superfluous here, the environment is hardly minimal. On every wall, in every corner, there is something surprising to look at: a bird's nest, a stone, a branch, a bone fragment, an extraordinary piece of wood, all arranged in a thoughtful, mindful manner. "I love nature. I might live in Manhattan, but I'm drawn to organic things," says Calero, who has an instinctual gift for placement and balance, symmetry and composition. "I like to live surrounded by these objects. I use them in my photographs, I put them away for a while; I love taking them out again and seeing them in a new way. "This loft is an honest space," she adds. "It's like me, it's my soul. I've always believed that the spaces you live in are like relationships. You just know when it's right."

OPPOSITE **Clockwise from far left, Calero's bed (reflected in the mirror) was made by Nakashima. In the bathroom, an oak sink and brushed-chrome fittings; the walls are covered in white subway tile. A mahogany shelf in the living area holds an ever-changing display of favorite artwork, objects, and ceramics.**

FOLLOWING PAGES **Clockwise from top left, a collection of wood platters and cutting boards in the kitchen. Linen-covered boxes are stacked on the library bookshelves. A Calero composition.**

design details

- I always have music playing; as soon as I walk in the door, I turn it on. And I listen to everything, anything that attracts my ear
- incense is always burning, you can smell its scent as soon as you exit the elevator. But no scented candles, it's so "in" to have candles and I don't want to be "in," so no candles
- I'm a Virgo and I love organization: everything goes into boxes and then comes out when I want to see it again. It's the way I edit my life
- I love looking at things in the flea market, I just don't buy it all. If something seems to say "take me home with you," I'll walk away from it and only go back if I'm still thinking about it later. If I feel some sort of connection, I know it's right
- I love the whole experience of the flea markets in France: at 11 in the morning, the dealers will break out their bottles of wine and baguettes, no matter what. It's a ritual; you have to love that
- I'm very aware when I'm walking outside. I'm always looking down on the ground and all around me, not just straight ahead. That's how I find these beautiful things in nature: branches, shells, leaves, bones, feathers. They're all there waiting to be discovered, and I'm so inspired by them

Graham Howe
Paul Outerbridge Jr: Photographs
AUGUSTE RODIN
PHAIDON

THE GIVENCHY STYLE
SNOWDON SITTINGS
SHOCK OF THE NEW
THE WATERWORKS
RFK
Georgia
ARCHITECTURE OF THE OLD SOUTH
PLAY FOOD
MATISSE

madelin

"The best part of being a designer," says Madeline Stuart, "is finding the right thing." And Stuart, a Los Angeles-based decorator known for the sophisticated rooms she creates for A-list Hollywood players, will search high and low to find—or create—a particular piece for a particular person. "Houses have to resonate with the sensibilities of the owners. If it's merely a reflection of me and my taste, they're not living in their house, they're living in mine."

Raised in Beverly Hills by a film-director father and interior-designer mother, Stuart says, "Hollywood is a place where reality is often transitory. In design, there's also an ideal of people living in a chic and elegant manner, living 'just so.' But real people don't live 'just so.' Real people get mail and catalogues that pile up and have junk drawers. The challenge is to help them live in a stylish way in a home that truly

e stuart

CRAK!
POUR LA FRANCE

works; I tend to try to do this with things that are a little more classic, a little more honest and time-honored."

Stuart's own home is a case in point. The designer, her writer husband, Steve Oney, and Jack Russell terrier, Jackson, recently moved to a 1931 Mediterranean-style house, built against a craggy granite hillside just above Hollywood. "There is a dramatic, slightly romantic aspect to this place," Stuart says. "It has all the features I love—a curving staircase, old wood floors, plaster walls, archways, and beautiful, original tilework. It reminds me that I live in L.A."

The spacious living room features a studied mix of old and new, where Stuart's furniture designs mingle happily with vintage stools and a remodeled 1956 Dunbar sofa passed down from her parents. True to her offbeat sensibility, the designer tucked a gold-leaf convex mirror and a bear skull into a niche set into the distinctive chimney. "I like to tweak convention," she says, "it makes a room seem not too sincere."

At the opposite end of the room, in front of an arched window, Stuart's nailhead-studded velvet sofa is flanked by her Hudson chairs. Wide archways lead to a sun porch painted in broad horizontal bands of subtle, earthy color and to Stuart's tailored home office, and, on the other side, to a dining room with windows dressed in billowing silk taffeta.

Stuart relaxes by cooking and gardening, and although her garden is still in its infancy, her kitchen is a gourmet's dream, with gleaming stainless-steel commercial-style appliances, limestone counters, and a cork floor. Her collections of antique Staffordshire china and ironstone serving pieces are stowed in a glass-front white cabinet. "I'm a hoarder," she says. "My china, my ironstone, my vintage glasses from the Paris flea market—I collect it and I use it. I love to cook and cook a real dinner every night with Steve. I just don't like kitchens that make too much of

PRECEDING PAGES **In the Hollywood Hills living room of Madeline Stuart and Steve Oney, Stuart's contemporary take on classic bergères and the Caroline tray table—an overscale tray set on an upholstered ottoman. She remodeled and recovered the vintage Dunbar sofa, a family heirloom; the vintage Thebes stools are lacquered Chinese red.**

OPPOSITE **The Roy Lichtenstein painting in the dining room was a gift from Stuart's father. She designed the dining-room table in mazzard wood—a European cherry—and dressed the windows in unlined silk taffeta; the vintage Louis XVI-style chairs have a painted finish and tied slipcovers.**

"I like to tweak convention; it makes
a room seem not too

sincere"

LEFT **The velvet-upholstered sofa at the far end of the living room is a Stuart design, as are the Hudson armchairs. The mirrored cocktail table is from the '40s; the ottoman is covered in a painterly Fortuny fabric.**

FOLLOWING PAGES **Clockwise from top left, Stuart's watercolor rendering of a chair design, and swatches and floor plan from a work in progress. In the sunporch at her house, the designer painted wide horizontal stripes in Donald Kaufman colors; the sycamore chair is an early piece by Christian Liaigre. The inspiration corkboard above Stuart's desk at her design firm.**

design details

- a good room needs a stripe. Striped fabric or wallpaper imbues an interior with a sense of humor, a sense of playfulness; there's one in every room I do
- I love old-fashioned, honest materials
- floors covered in cork are incredible, it's the material of the moment. It's soft and warm, you can stand on it for hours, and it's a renewable resource
- things made by hand have enormous value to them. I particularly love my stationery: it's letter-pressed by hand on antique machines
- quirky, slightly macabre bits and pieces—like my bear skull, or framed insects from Deyrolle in Paris—that are just odd enough to make someone slightly discomfited, keep a room from being too staid
- I don't like things that are overly matched. I don't tend to do a room based on a single color scheme or key fabric
- tile wainscoting—installed at least 42 inches up a wall—is a gracious detail that adds character to a bathroom

Elliott Erwitt | Personal Exposures
the sixties

themselves. A kitchen should work, period. It doesn't need to be a major fashion statement."

Upstairs, the master bedroom "was built for twin beds flanking the window," Stuart laughs. "There's no other bed wall. It must have been very Lucy and Ricky Ricardo, the Hayes Act of architecture. But even with our bed in front of the window, we are still able to look out onto the most extraordinary steep hillside covered in brush and plumbago trees."

"I finally realized you can't just unpack all your things from your old house and put them in the new house," Stuart says. "You have to allow yourself to evolve and change, to readjust your vision and improve your design vocabulary. We all get a little bit stuck; it took this new house to make me see things with a new clarity."

ABOVE **The walls in Stuart's dressing room are painted pale pink. A Regency mirror from her childhood bedroom is flanked by a pair of 1930s crystal lamps.** OPPOSITE **The bedroom overlooks a steep hillside covered in brush and plumbago trees. The bed is a Stuart design, outfitted with antique and vintage linens; the mohair throw is by Hermès.**

victo

Cool, cerebral, orderly, suffused with light: Victoria Hagan's signature style is perfectly balanced but not obsessed with getting everything precisely right. "Rooms need spontaneity and imperfection," the New York City designer says, "because we don't live in a perfect world."

This attitude explains the eclecticism of Hagan's Park Avenue apartment, which she shares with her media-executive husband, Michael Berman, and their five-year-old twin boys. Its prewar neoclassical scale is loosened up by a generosity of spirit, an appreciation for the whimsies of style combined with practical common sense. "It's not about Mommy's apartment," she says with a laugh. "It's a family apartment; the boys can go everywhere."

And that means serious fun, though with an urban edge. For Hagan, great design cannot be separated from geography, a lesson she learned

ria hagan

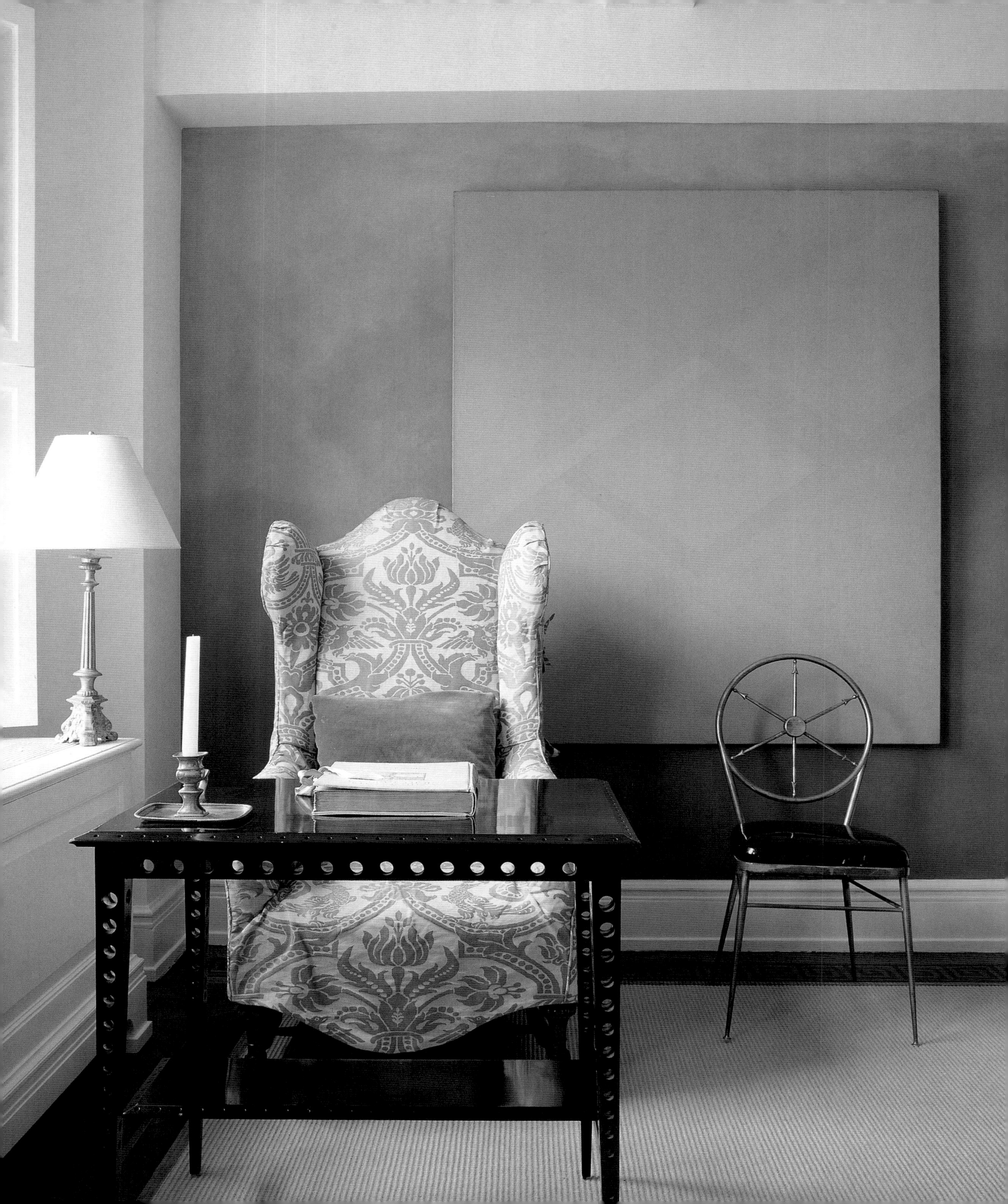

starting out with her mentor, the late designer Simone Feldman. Authenticity is key. "If you're in the country or at the beach, the house should look like you're in the country or at the beach, not in another country," she says.

Painted aged white and accented with fabrics and finishes in foggy shades of gray, putty, cream, blue, and chocolate punctuated by black and gold, the space is a sexy collage of countries, styles, and textures. The rich but muted color scheme, for instance, came from the palette of the nineteenth-century French painter Ingres. "The world is full of inspiration," she says, "from the color of freshly picked corn-on-the-cob to something I've seen in a museum, or a set in a movie."

Hagan's preference is for the big mix, her curious mind reflected in juxtapositions that range from charming to startling. In the living room, a reproduction of a chair by the great early nineteenth-century neoclassicist Thomas Hope, for example, keeps company with a white chair of molded Fiberglas from the 1963 New York World's Fair. "I think that plastic chair made the room sing," she says. Alongside the sleek Florence Knoll cocktail table is a funky butterfly stool of leather and twisted wire. In the bedroom, Hagan dispensed with the traditional headboard; instead, she filled the wall above the bed with large gilt-framed canvases of cavorting nymphs.

"I took a few more chances here than I would with a client," she admits. Motherhood dictated some choices, too. Sisal-look carpeting made of hard-wearing wool paves the floors, although it's bound with velvet in the living room. And accessories lean toward the unbreakable: brass candlesticks, a gold-leafed bronze bowl. "Since I had the boys, I'm into metal a lot more," Hagan adds. "And although I love luxury and beautiful things, I tend to shy away from ostentation. Precious things

PRECEDING PAGE **In Victoria Hagan's Park Avenue living room, an eighteenth-century painting in the style of Canaletto, a 1950s Florence Knoll laminate-and-steel cocktail table, and a sofa of her own design, upholstered in pale ocher fine-wale corduroy.**

OPPOSITE **A slipcovered antique wing chair, 1920s French pierced-metal table, vintage brass Gio Ponti side chair with a black patent-leather seat, and a painting by Donald Kaufman.**

ABOVE AND OPPOSITE **In the library, Hagan plays with the scale of a Greek-key design in a graphic carpet and the carved edge of a neoclassic pedestal table that extends for dining. The library sofa was inspired by a famous suede-covered original owned by Coco Chanel; Hagan dressed her homage in charcoal wool. The 1960s cocktail table is a studded leather-covered Parsons table; the painting is by David Hacker.**

make me a nervous wreck, and it's because of me, not my children."

The result is an environment that is stylish but not fussy. The creative impulse was not how well the place would showcase Hagan's work but how easily it could be lived in. Her mantra? "Keep it real, keep it honest. When in doubt, keep it simple."

“Rooms need spontaneity

and imperfection"

LEFT **Hagan replaced the original mantel with a more substantial classically styled one and juxtaposed a steel-framed mirror with the antique French living room mantel clock; she painted the walls flanking the fireplace a stormy gray. A neo-Egyptian armchair, one of a pair, is upholstered in silk velvet; the white molded-Fiberglas chair is from the 1963 New York World's Fair.**

FOLLOWING PAGES **From left, an Empire-style bedside table and Venetian-glass lamp. The 1920's painted Swedish-style cabinet hides the television, the brass sunburst mirror is from the '50s. An industrial-steel desk lamp, plaster maquette of a horse, and 1940s Italian shield-back chair.**

design details

- light is the most important thing to me. I always want a sense of daylight in a room, even if I have to create it
- I love seasonal flowers: if it's spring, I want it to look like spring. And if the flowers have a strong scent, all the better. Rooms should smell wonderful
- I like to play with scale and composition. Mixing proportion, style, and provenance creates an element of surprise
- I'm a good listener—every designer should be—and I have learned a great deal from my clients
- living rooms should be designed so you can comfortably seat large groups of people. Four to six is easy, it's seating ten that's difficult
- production is so important. You can have the greatest ideas in the world, but they're futile if you can't get them produced. I have a terrific staff and a great team of craftsmen; I'd be lost without them
- steadfast rules are meant to be broken: an unexpected touch adds energy to a space
- the best design ideas come from experience

page goo

"I'm not a minimalist by any means," says Manhattan-based architect Page Goolrick, just a touch defensively, "but I feel strongly about design that works." Her own home is a case in point. Dividing time between residential and commercial projects, Goolrick runs her small firm out of the SoHo loft where she both lives and works. The space has a strong element of restraint, but while minimalism often denotes a coldly stark interior, devoid of the human touch, Goolrick's live/work environment is refreshingly intimate, filled with warmth and light and dramatic city views.

It is efficient, too. Client meetings take place in a sun-splashed conference room that does double-duty as a kitchen, with hidden storage and hinged counters that flip up to reveal appliances. "I've thrown dinner parties for twelve here," Goolrick

lrick

December
F S S
4 5 6
11 12 13
18 19 20
25

says, "that haven't been compromised by the fact that it's also a conference room." The office library by day becomes the living/sleeping area at night, thanks to a Murphy bed and a clever five-by-eight-foot pivoting panel that closes off the rest of the loft to provide a sense of privacy.

Goolrick's apartment is intelligent design at its best, a stylish solution to common space-constraint problems. In fact, many clients, particularly commercial ones, don't know it's her home. "It's a live/work space that nobody realizes is a live/work space," she says. "I don't want to appear to be a woman working at home, and this place certainly doesn't scream 'home.'"

"I'm always trying to simplify," Goolrick says. "I interview my clients extensively when I take on a project and study their wants and needs; sometimes I think I'm actually more of an efficiency expert." Inspired by reductivist masters such as Richard Neutra, Walter Gropius, Le Corbusier, and Charles and Ray Eames, Goolrick favors "honest" materials—steel, concrete, wood, marble, and glass. She often develops her own product designs and has created an extensive line of lighting with distinctive shades of stainless-steel mesh. She says, "I like to use at least one unique, project-specific invention in each job."

An avid sailor, Goolrick says her sailboat racing has informed her creativity. "It's strengthened my feelings about architecture and design," she says. "Boat design is very specific: many things have dual functions and everything you use is stowed in a specially designed place. I try to apply those principles to my residential work: living in a well-designed place makes living there so much better."

PRECEDING PAGE **In the living area/library of Page Goolrick's SoHo loft, a flea-market sofa that she reconstructed and recovered, a credenza by American modernist Florence Knoll, and *Clocktower*, a silkscreen by Lorna Simpson. Goolrick installed a Murphy bed on the opposite wall.**

OPPOSITE **Goolrick designed frameless steel-and-glass doors to separate the office area from the conference room/kitchen. The door on the far wall pivots to close off the library (by day) and living area/bedroom (by night).**

"It's a live/work space that nobody re

alizes is a live/work space"

LEFT **When not hosting clients, the conference room turns into a kitchen: cleverly designed cabinetry conceals an oven, dishwasher, and washer/dryer; the counters are hinged to flip up and provide easy access. The maple table and stainless-steel mesh light fixtures are Goolrick designs.**

FOLLOWING PAGES **Clockwise from bottom left, some of Goolrick's lighting designs. A collage of favorite construction materials. Goolrick designed the Jean-Michel Frank–inspired sofa and upholstered it in wool by Donghia; a translucent door slides in front of the shelves to hide catalogues and sourcebooks. Goolrick's well-organized desktop.**

design details

- my motto: "simplify, simplify, simplify"
- I prefer balance to symmetry, which can be too rigid or confining
- so much of architecture is what you don't see; it's what makes a space truly efficient
- if you can streamline or simplify an activity—finding your keys or dressing in the morning—you can use your saved time to do something more enjoyable
- minimal needn't imply empty; it can just be a straightforward, well thought-out space
- simple, honest materials usually age with grace: concrete is very forgiving, marble develops a lovely patina, and the first scratch in stainless steel is the worst—the surface becomes more beautiful with time

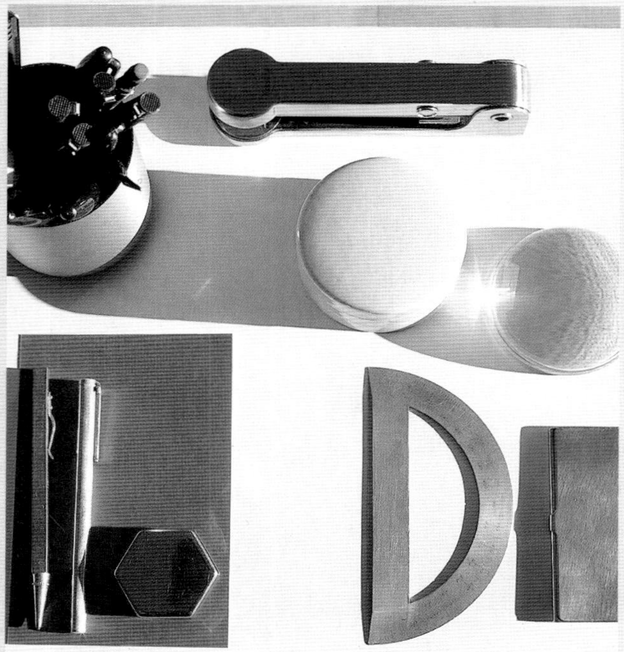

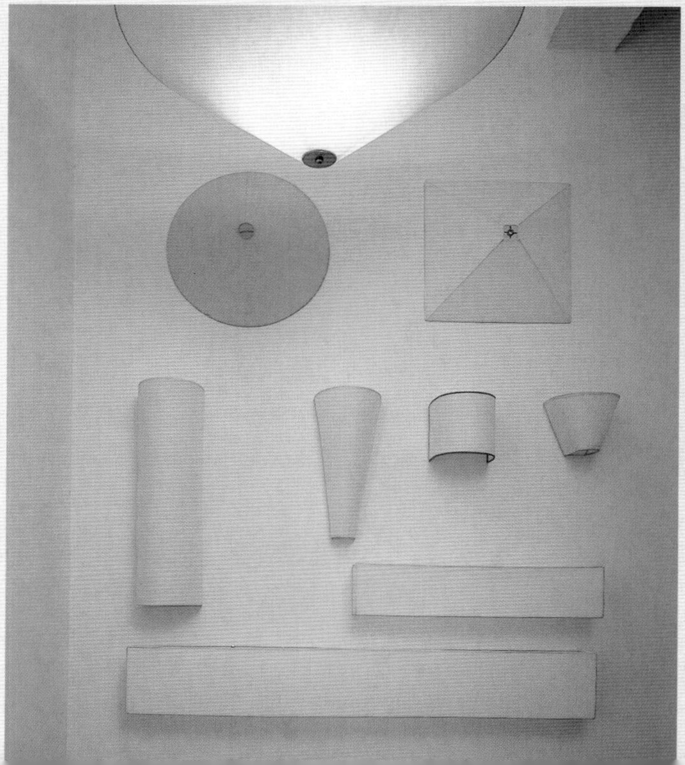

BENDHEIM
CONSTANTINE
CARPET
FABRIC
WALL COVER
SAILCLOTH

charlotte

Virginia-born Charlotte Moss spent a full ten years as a Wall Street marketing executive before capitulating to her real love, interior design. As the owner of an eponymous shop that sold antiques, decorative accessories, and furniture for eleven years (since shuttered), Moss built a roster of high-profile clients, then went on to design collections of furniture and accessories, create "Virginia"—a signature home fragrance—write best-selling design books, and hit the lecture circuit. Since closing her boutique, she has concentrated on decorating projects, product design, and consulting; she is currently under contract as an advisor to the Colonial Williamsburg Foundation.

Highly energized yet surprisingly not high-strung, Moss can expound on a wide variety of subjects with a contagious enthusiasm. The homes she creates—for clients and for her family—are as

moss

Perennial
Garden
MONTAGUE FREE
FLOWER DECORATION
I'M IN
THE GARDEN

compelling as the stories she tells, rich in the detail that makes interiors more interesting and life more comfortable. Deeply cushioned sofas and chairs are inviting, reading lamps with her trademark pleated-silk shades provide soft lighting, bedrooms are dressed with luxurious linens and scented candles, and baths are designed with the most modern yet classically styled fittings.

Moss is a professional, clearly attuned to the importance of subtleties. Extraordinary attention to detail and execution is at the core of her work. The designer's father had been in the military, and she says, "He always asked 'What's the plan?' no matter what had to be done. I think that's constantly in the back of my mind, to have a plan that works."

A plan, yes, a formula, no. Moss has written, "Decorating . . . is one of the most personal activities we can pursue. It's a form of self-expression. There are no formulas, no special magic, no right or wrong way." Once pigeonholed as a purveyor of the cozy, English-country-house style, Moss's tastes today are wider in scope. "I use everything—English, French, and Italian furniture," she says. "I don't decorate by geography." She alludes to diverse inspirations, from eighteenth-century architects and craftsmen to fashion designers Claire McCardell and Cristobal Balenciaga. Strongly influenced by stylish women of the twentieth century, Moss designed a furniture collection paying homage to Coco Chanel, Lady Sibyl Colefax, Lady Diana Cooper, the Duchess of Windsor, and Elsie de Wolfe.

"I like to create rooms that are elegant, but comfortable," Moss says. "That regardless of how much money has been spent on a place, it doesn't have that off-putting, formal edge to it. I think it's my Southern heritage: if I invite someone over, I want them to feel at ease the moment they walk in."

PRECEDING PAGE **The screened porch in Charlotte Moss and Barry Friedberg's East Hampton house features a river-stone fireplace and Bar Harbor wicker furniture painted a sophisticated black.**

OPPOSITE **The former service entrance, a long passageway leading from the garage to the kitchen, was transformed into a flower room. Moss contructed special storage for flower containers, garden pots, baskets, potting soil, and tools. The wainscoting and shelves are painted a glazed celadon; the counters are pewter.**

ABOVE **Moss streaked and glazed the pool house's pine walls gray to resemble driftwood. The desk is a galvanized-steel-topped potting table from Mecox Gardens; the framed engravings are of garden structures and follies.**
OPPOSITE **The view over the pool toward the main house; the pool house is at the far end of the pool.**

Moss and her husband, investment banker Barry Friedberg, own homes in Manhattan and Aspen and recently purchased a house in Los Angeles, but it's their compound in East Hampton, Long Island where they relax and entertain friends on summer weekends. "It's funny," Moss says, "this was not the kind of house I was looking for. I wanted an old shingle-style place but found this one—basically a late 1980s 'spec' house—on a terrific piece of land and realized we could make it into what we needed."

Today, the house is a beautifully landscaped, classic shingled structure. The couple has been doctoring it for fifteen years, adding architectural detail, balance and symmetry, and lush gardens with the

help of architect Dale Booher and landscape designer Lisa Stamm. They built a screened porch—"It's the connection to the outside and is where we really live," says Moss—with an old-fashioned sleeping porch and home office upstairs. The double-height living room features floor-to-ceiling bookcases filled with design books and vintage fashion and decorating magazines. In the dining room, the designer paired an English table with French chairs and, in the summery master suite, installed trellis-pattern wallpaper and a tester bed dressed in floral prints. A service passage was converted to a flower room, and a media room, home gym, wine cellar, and large laundry room (a necessity with the couple's entertaining schedule) were added as well.

The designer's touch is also evident outside the main house, where the gardens and plantings were inspired by those Moss has seen in books and in her travels. "The tennis court, pool, and pool house were existing," she says, "but other than a few oaks and pear trees, there wasn't one stick! We followed Gertrude Jekyll's lead and planted climbers to grow up the tree trunks—climbing hydrangea, variegated ivy, and clematis—it makes the gardens look so much more lush."

Moss tries to take long weekends and books nearby client appointments on Fridays so she has Saturday and Sunday free. Although active in local charities, Moss says, "I don't feel compelled to go to every charity 'do'; I'm just not out here to be so social." She prefers to have girlfriends to lunch, and the couple has a few dinner parties each season. Otherwise, Friedberg golfs and Moss scouts the antiques fairs or putters in the garden, and sometimes they go kayaking on nearby Georgica Pond. "We live on a cul-de-sac," Moss says. "It's so private, it feels like it's at the end of the world, not at all what you think about the Hamptons. This place is our own little club."

OPPOSITE **Clockwise from top left, an antique apple-picking ladder stands just inside the gate at the back entrance of the property. A rustic bench and Virginia-creeper-covered trellis. Moss assembled obelisks and pots and planters filled with lush plants outside the kitchen. An antique English sundial in the kitchen garden.**

FOLLOWING PAGES **From left, Moss found the lavender tablecloth and napkins at a flea market and had them monogrammed. Passion fruit sorbet. The table is set for lunch with lavender linens, mixed antique Staffordshire china atop rattan chargers, French flatware made of rosewood and silver, reproduction Regency crystal by William Yeoward, and a centerpiece of flowers from the garden.**

design details

- when working on a design project, build a notebook of floor plans and swatches for each room. Keep a record of measurements and add snapshots of furniture and accessories you've bought
- let your interiors evolve with you—they should reflect the changes in your life. Don't be afraid to experiment, to move things around from room to room. Paint the walls or slipcover a chair; decoration shouldn't be static. Take risks
- I collect vintage fashion and decorating magazines and just bound all my old *Vogues* in red leather. If you collect design magazines, stack them on your shelves alongside your books
- don't overwhelm your bookshelves with *objets*. A picture or vase tucked here and there might add interest, but the books should come first
- keep a scrapbook of pictures of rooms or objects you're drawn to in your travels: favorite table settings, a detail of a skirt on a chair, the way a bed has been made
- when setting a table, mix china patterns the way you might mix antiques and add unexpected small accessories to decorate the table
- always have something with a bit of history in a room. If everything is new, the decor looks like it was done overnight, not over time

"It's my Southern heritage:
over, I want them to feel at ease the

if I invite someone
moment they walk in"

LEFT **Moss's glorious old-fashioned roses include damasks and gallicas; on the far side of the swimming pool, climbing 'New Dawn' roses grow on tuteurs at the rear of the perennial garden.**

sourcebook

Muriel Brandolini

Muriel Brandolini Inc.
212-249-4920

For Muriel Brandolini tabletop accessories and fashion:
Barneys New York
For stores: 888-8-BARNEYS

For Muriel Brandolini fabrics:
Travers & Co. (open to the trade only)
For showrooms: 212-888-7900

Black lacquer tables and antiques from:
Madeleine Castaing
30 rue Jacob
Paris 75006 France
011-331-43-54-91-71

For carpets:
Allegra Hicks
2/27 Chelsea Harbour Design Centre
London SW10 OXE England
011-44-207-351-9696

Sheila Bridges

Sheila Bridges Design, Inc.
1925 Seventh Avenue
New York, NY 10026
212-678-6872
www.sheilabridges.com

For antiques, furniture, and accessories:
Sheila Bridges Home, Inc.
610 Warren Street
Hudson, NY 12534
518-822-9724

For lighting:
Lampa
631-722-9450
www.lampa.com

My favorite flea market:
The Annex 26th Street Flea Market
Every Saturday and Sunday
9 A.M.–5 P.M.
26th Street and Avenue of the Americas
New York, NY 10001
212-243-5343

For sisal carpet:
Sisal Direct
888-613-1335
www.sisalrugs.com

Anita Calero

For antique textiles:
Cora Ginsburg
212-744-1352

For carpets:
Dolma
417 Lafayette Street
New York, NY 10003
212-460-5525

For contemporary furniture and accessories:
Moss
146 Greene Street
New York, NY 10012
212-226-2190

Mariette Himes Gomez

Mariette Himes Gomez Associates, Inc.
506 East 74th Street
New York, NY 10021
212-288-6856

For custom-colored paint:
Donald Kaufman Color Factory
For information: 201-568-2226

For furniture and art:
Doyle New York
175 East 87th Street
New York, NY 10028
212-427-2730

For housewares:
Crate & Barrel
For information: 800-996-9960

Page Goolrick

Page Goolrick Architects
110 Greene Street
New York, NY 10012
212-219-3666

For architectural glass:
Bendheim
122 Hudson Street
New York, NY 10013
212-226-6370

For nautical hardware:
Ronstan
ronstanusa@aol.com

For light-fixture components:
Grand Brass Lamp Parts
221 Grand Street
New York, NY 10013
212-226-2567

Tricia Guild

Designers Guild
265 Kings Road
London SW3 England
011-44-207-351-5775

For Designers Guild fabric and wallpaper:
Osborne & Little (open to the trade only)
979 Third Avenue
New York, NY 10022
For showrooms: 212-751-3333

Victoria Hagan

Victoria Hagan Interiors
654 Madison Avenue
New York, NY 10021
212-888-1178

For carpets:
A.M. Collections
584 Broadway
New York, NY 10012
212-625-2616

For antiques:
Yew Tree House Antiques
414 East 71st Street
New York, NY 10021
212-249-6612

Holly Hunt

Holly Hunt (open to the trade only)
1728 Merchandise Mart
Chicago, IL 60654
312-661-1900

Holly Hunt New York
(open to the trade only)
979 Third Avenue
New York, NY 10022
212-755-6555

For flowers, accessories, tabletop accessories, and linens:
Takashimaya
693 Fifth Avenue
New York, NY 10022
212-350-0100

For antiques:
Ciancimino
99 Pimlico Road
London SW1 England
011-44-207-730-9950

Kathryn Ireland

Kathryn M. Ireland, Inc.
1619 Stanford Street
Santa Monica, CA 90404
310-315-4351

For Kathryn Ireland fabrics:
Hollyhock Hilldale
817 N. Hilldale Avenue
West Hollywood, CA 90069
310-777-0100

John Rosselli & Associates
(open to the trade only)
979 Third Avenue
New York, NY 10022
212-593-2060

For traditional lamps and lighting fixtures:
Vaughan Designs, Inc.
(open to the trade only)
979 Third Avenue
New York, NY 10022
212-319-7070

For plumbing fixtures:
Waterworks
For store information: 800-899-6757
www.waterworks.com

Catherine Memmi

Catherine Memmi
34 rue Saint-Sulpice
Paris 75006 France
011-331-44-07-22-28

Galerie Catherine Memmi
11 rue Saint-Sulpice
Paris 75006 France

Les Basiques de Catherine Memmi
43 rue Madame
Paris 75006 France

Charlotte Moss

Charlotte Moss & Co.
16 East 65th Street
New York, NY 10021
212-772-6244

For trees, plants, books, and garden furniture and accessories:
Mecox Gardens
257 County Road 39A
Southampton, NY 11969
631-287-5015
Call for other store locations.

For crystal glassware:
William Yeoward Crystal
For stores: 800-818-8484

For home fragrance:
Jo Malone
949 Broadway
New York, NY 10010
For information: 212-572-4200

Liz O'Brien

Liz O'Brien
800A Fifth Avenue
New York, NY 10021
212-755-3800

For vintage furniture:
Galerie de Beyrie
393 West Broadway
New York, NY 10012
212-219-9565

Alan Moss
436 Lafayette Street
New York, NY 10003
212-473-1310

For design books, both new and out-of-print:
Archivia
944 Madison Avenue
New York, NY 10021
212-439-9194

Ellen O'Neill

Ralph Lauren Home
For stores and information: 800-578-7656 or 212-642-8700

For vintage fashion and design magazines:
Gallagher Paper Collectibles
126 East 12th Street
New York, NY 10003
212-473-2404

For antiques:
Paula Rubenstein
65 Prince Street
New York, NY 10012
212-966-8954

Historical Materialism
125 Crosby Street
New York, NY 10012
212-431-3424

Sage Street Antiques
Sage Street and Route 114
Sag Harbor, NY 11963
631-725-4036

Suzanne Rheinstein

Suzanne Rheinstein Associates
310-550-8900

Hollyhock
214 N. Larchmont Boulevard
Los Angeles, CA 90004
323-931-3400

Hollyhock Hilldale
817 N. Hilldale Avenue
West Hollywood, CA 90069
310-777-0100

For antiques:
J.F. Chen
8414 Melrose Avenue
West Hollywood, CA 90069
323-655-6310

For garden antiques and accessories:
Treillage
418 East 75th Street
New York, NY 10021
212-535-2288

For furniture, accessories, and antiques:
Yeoward South
The Old Imperial Laundry
71 Warriner Gardens
London SW11 4XW England
011-44-207-498-4811

Madeline Stuart

Madeline Stuart & Associates, Inc.
630 S. La Brea Avenue
Los Angeles, CA 90036
323-935-3305

For hand-printed letterpress stationery:
Zida Borchich Letterpress
711 N. Main Street
Fort Bragg, CA 95437
707-964-2522

For vintage hardware:
Liz's Antique Hardware
453 S. La Brea Avenue
Los Angeles, CA 90036
323-939-4403

For Tibetan carpets:
Aga John
8687 Melrose Avenue
Los Angeles, CA 90069
310-657-0890

Celia Tejada

Pottery Barn
For store/catalogue information:
800-922-9934
www.potterybarn.com

For collectibles:
Alabaster
597 Hayes Street
San Francisco, CA 94102
415-558-0482

For my favorite Merlot:
Miura Vineyards
Napa Valley, CA
800-500-3142

For decorative accessories:
Fillamento
2185 Fillmore Street
San Francisco, CA 94115
415-931-2224